I find Mary Ellen's new devotional refreshing for each of us who encounter the daily struggle to reflect Christ in a world of difficulties, challenges, and weariness. Always pointing the reader to Christ, she encourages us to choose gratefulness, self⸳⸳⸳ ⸳nd joy in our responses to life's circumstancᵉˢ ⸳⸳he narrow way to the abundant lifᵉ ⸳⸳⸳

The glimpses into her life a⸳ are an intriguing and enriching and think beyond our own cul⸳ ⸳ighly recommend this book for both yᴏ ⸳⸳ᴄᴇ.

–Evelyn Miller, Author, *Feminine Beauty*

Mary Ellen has lovingly prepared a nourishing stew of devotional morsels from the gardens of her life. Two gardens 10,000 miles apart—the slums of Africa and the hills of Ohio. Dipping into the hearty mixture, the next bite may be a spicy Kenyan anecdote or homegrown goodness from Ohio's Amish Country.

Simmering in a base of passion for God and truth and peppered with exhortation, the nuggets Mary Ellen has collected along her journey nourish the hearts of girls and women in varied life stages and circumstances.

–Dorcas Hoover, Author, *House Calls and Hitching Posts*

Mary Ellen's encouraging voice calls women of all ages and stations toward a greater devotion to God. She applies the wisdom she has learned from Him and His people and brings it to bear on stories from her years in Africa and America. I am inspired by Mary Ellen's assurance that, though cultures differ, attitudes are universal, and the source of Light is changeless on every continent. Under her quiet guidance, I felt myself leaning toward Him.

–Sheila Petre, Author, *Thirty Little Fingers*

Leaning

TOWARD

the Light

Finding Joy in Difficult Places

Mary Ellen Beachy

DEDICATION

For Lorene
who models
Love, life and care
Pouring out herself
For Jesus
In the ER
Caring for her parents
And for many friends
Of all ages
In foreign lands
And at home.

Christ shall give thee LIGHT.

EPHESIANS 5:14

THE LIGHT

The golden sun rays
Warm and brighten
The waiting earth
Each morning.

As I turn to Jesus
His light and love
Diffuse dark doubts
And gray shadows.

He gives morning joy,
Warm light, love
And fresh hope
For every new day.

Contents

Introduction: Leaning Toward the Light   1

A Difficult First Week   3

Welcome the Children   5

Keep No Record   7

Grumbling Missionaries   9

More of God's Presence   11

A Gracious Mother-in-Law   13

Show Kindness   15

In the Night Watches   17

Do Not Be Afraid   19

One May Day in Kenya   21

Together Fifty Years   23

Heart Longings   25

An Hour for Beauty   27

What If?   29

Open Gates   31

Walls and Gates   33

Look Your Child in the Eye   35

This Mother-in-Law Thing   37

Choose Love   39

Calm Commitment   41

Support Him   43

Women's Fears   45

Grateful or Not   47

Guidance and Protection   49
When Danger Threatens   51
Many Prayers in Kenya   53
Boldness   55
Forgive Him   57
Encouraging Josephine   59
A Big Heart   61
My Friends, Kenyan Ladies   63
Never Lose Hope   65
Remember Jesus   67
Cared For   69
Only in Africa   71
What Kind of Visitor?   73
Church Cultures   75
My Beautiful Cousin   77
Make God Big   79
Love Connections   81
Warmed by Kindness   83
The Sad Old Man   85
What Do You Want?   87
No Greater Joy   89
Meaningful Ways   91
Refreshed   93
Enjoyed, Shocked   95
Summer Fruits   97
My Lovely Friend   99
Time to Nurture   101
A Mother-in-Law Manual   103
Life Overseas   105
Edifying Books   107
Be an Encourager   109
Influence Others   111
Seize Opportunities   113

Remote Places	115
Her Canon of Praise	117
In Quiet Days	119
Snapshots of Kenya	121
One Drumstick	123
Singing on the Couch	125
Yes Woman	127
God My Refuge	129
Babies and Beads	131
Changes and Tears	133
Pleasant and Green	135
Serve My Generation	137
A Daughter's Vigil	139
A Big "Praise the Lord"	141
Barns and Treasures	143
Accepted	145
Stories	147
That Monster	149
Small Prayers, A Big God	151
Shriveled	153
Washed My Feet	155
Walking on Water	157
Long Visits	159
Write an E-Mail	161
My Hard Heart	163
My Neighbor	165
Called to Love	167
All-Night Wake	169
Why Did He Weep?	171
Burnout	173
Oh Mary Don't You Weep	175
Lose Your Focus	177
I'm Raising Boys	179

Leave Beauty 181

Mother's Reflections 183

A Living Sacrifice 185

Where I Am 187

Warm and Welcoming 189

So Low 191

Kenya Again 193

He Weeps; He Cares 195

Too Comfortable 197

Never Alone 199

Africa and America 201

Epilogue: Rest in Life's Seasons 203

INTRODUCTION

Leaning Toward the Light

Nearly half of the devotionals throughout this book are from my family's days serving as missionaries in Kenya. I hope that sharing my struggles and joys will encourage women now serving God in other lands. The other entries are from life in our homeland, before and after Africa.

What I needed for joy and fulfillment in a foreign land, a living, loving relationship with Jesus, is what I also need at home.

The Light of the world is Jesus.

By the big window in our family room, I placed some small seedlings. Tiny plants need much light to grow well. In the evening, I placed a lighted lamp beside the seedlings, and the next morning, when I checked the plants, I was amazed. Each little plant was leaning toward the light.

Jesus is my light; His words are Life. Am I leaning toward the light each day?

Today there are so many voices calling.

There is so much to fill my mind and my time.

Will I take time for what truly matters?

Will I fill my mind with Jesus . . .

With His life, peace, and joy?

Wherever I live, wherever I work, I need Jesus. He said:

"I am the way, the truth, and the life" (John 14:6)"

"Attend to my words; incline thine ear unto my sayings. Let them not depart from thine eyes; keep them in the midst of thine heart. For they are *life* unto those that find them, and health to all their flesh" (Proverbs 4:20-22).

Jesus deserves all praise and glory. Thank Jesus if what I write encourages you or does any good.

Life is a challenge wherever we live. There will be trials and struggles until we get home. Through it all, I am grateful God is with me. The Light of the world is Jesus. I want to share His Light and love.

Mary Ellen

A Difficult
First Week

I cried unto the LORD with my voice,
and he heard me out of his holy hill. –Psalm 3:4

The first seven days in Kenya are over. They were difficult days. I had not expected such a big adjustment. The first week we were thrown into five days of language study. That about did me in. I was trying to unpack and make a home in this house. I had to cook for our sons while adjusting to cooking without my freezers and canning shelves full of food. What was I to cook? The local food seemed strange. All of that *Yet there is* plus no old friends to keep us company . . . and *sunshine.* the language study was trying.

Then Saturday evening, to top off everything, a son got sick and threw up viciously. *He needs Your healing touch, Jesus.* When my sons hurt, I hurt. Many visitors and new people get sick while adjusting to Africa. Germs lurk, especially in food and water sources.

On the day before Christmas, the five of us, Mark and I and our three sons, went shopping at Nakumatt, a modern store in Kisumu. The store was full; a sea of black people surrounded us. I found chocolates for Christmas and cool mugs with African animals for our sons. We also purchased mosquito nets. I will sleep better without those pesky critters whining in my ear, as I often cannot fall asleep quickly. The bar music is loud and throbbing, the ungodly pounding filling our house and head. Our sofa and our mattress are so firm. There are so many new people and strange new ways, plus the discouraging, exhausting fatigue from jet lag.

Yet there is sunshine:

- Marcellus went on a walk with me around the city block Sunday morning. He related a dream.
- Markus and Micah walked with Dean's boys to the Animal Market. They came home with carved African animals, some made of wood and others of soapstone. I was grateful to see them happy.
- Markus memorized Psalm 30. He recited it word-perfect.
- On the way home from Bible Study, God graced the sky with a perfect, brilliant rainbow. It was a day-brightener, an assurance of God with us. Micah went to get the red wagon at Weaver's to haul jugs of purified water to our house. He returned with four little boys on the wagon. He took time for them, and that blessed my heart. Small Levi started to cry, so I ran out with Smarties to cheer him.

Jesus, help me. I must look for blessings through
all of these looming adjustments.

Read Romans 8:28-39

Welcome the Children

But Jesus called them unto him, and said, Suffer little children to come unto me, and forbid them not; for of such is the kingdom of God. –Luke 18:16

Jesus took time for children. I love the account in Mark 10. Jesus had big things and important missions to accomplish. Yet He opened his arms to children, much to the disciples' chagrin. They thought the Master was too busy to bother with small ones.

Am I willing to take time and bless small children, whether it's my own grandchildren or others? I want the children and their mothers to know I love them. My heart is warmed when children run to me. I like it when they ask their mom if they can sit with me in church.

Jesus had big things and important missions to accomplish. Yet He opened his arms to children, much to the disciples' chagrin.

I love to read the Word before I face the day. One morning while we were visiting our daughter in Kansas, I read Mark 9 and wrote in my journal, "Welcome little children in Jesus's name." Just then I heard the pitter-patter of small feet coming down the stairs. In popped our three-year-old grandson, comically clothed with a warm cap and jacket, yet barefooted. I smiled and told him he could go up to get a book so we could have a story. He happily ran off and returned, clutching a book.

His little sister popped into the room as well. At first, she wasn't sure about joining us, but then she propped herself cozily against the pillows as we read and sang. I seldom get to babysit these dear children. It was a joy to open my arms and welcome them.

Years ago, one of our minister's wives remembered our children's birthdays with a card and a small gift. A single girl in our church paid attention to and loved our children. A schoolteacher from another state would visit and bring books for them. All of these friends blessed my days and brightened the lives of my children.

Welcome the children. Love them. It is important that each of them receives attention, warmth, and welcome in our homes, in church, and wherever we meet the precious little ones Jesus loves. If children and youth do not feel care, welcome, and friendliness at church, they might walk out those church doors as adults and not return.

Will we welcome the children? Will we take time
to be an influence for Jesus in their lives?

Read Mark 10:13-15

Keep No Record

And forgive us our debts, as we forgive our debtors.
–Matthew 6:12

A certain lady was new in missions in a foreign land. As is the case far too often, there was a woman with whom she needed to work who annoyed her frequently.

On a small writing tablet, this new lady, who really wanted to serve the Lord, kept a written record of the things this woman was doing that irritated her. *She is not friendly. She has all the answers. She is critical of new people.* Whenever something happened that to her mind was not good about this woman, she carefully wrote it down in fine script.

Reading the Word was something the new lady loved. Each morning, as she studied the Living Word, she heard the sounds of a city coming to life: children crying, people talking, the Muslim call to prayer sounding its daily ritual, and the beep-beeping of the three-wheeled *tuk tuks* filling the morning air with a kaleidoscope of aural colors. She truly wanted God to speak to her heart, and to live in a way that pleased Him.

Love is a choice.

But one morning the Lord stopped her in her tracks.

Her heart was touched as she read about love in 1 Corinthians 13. She read verses 4-5, "Love is patient and kind. Love is not jealous or boastful or proud or rude. It does not demand its own way. It is not irritable." The rest of that verse leapt off the page and hit her in the face: "IT KEEPS NO RECORD OF BEING WRONGED" (NLT).

There it was. Those words . . . "love keeps no record of being wronged." What should she do? What would she do? She got off her chair, found her little tablet with the list of perceived wrongs, ripped out that page, and hurled it into the trash.

She prayed for God to give her love and power to live His Word in a practical, obedient way.

Love is a choice. Love is not just a warm feeling. She would choose to live out love.

To those who wrong and hurt us, may we remember Jesus's words in Matthew 5:44: "But I say unto you, Love your enemies, bless them that curse you, do good to them that hate you, and pray for them which despitefully use you, and persecute you; that ye may be the children of your Father which is in heaven."

Lord, I want to love, bless, do good, and pray.
Show me the way, this very day.

Read 1 Corinthians 13

Grumbling Missionaries

*For every creature of God is good, and nothing to be refused,
if it be received with thanksgiving: For it is sanctified by the
word of God and prayer.* –1 Timothy 4:4-5

ew cultures and foods are fun and exciting when you are traveling in a foreign country for only a short time. But when time stretches into days, months, and years, there can be many adjustments, grumblings, and tears. There is nothing wrong with tears or adjustments. Adjusting takes time. Give yourself time. Crying to God to see you through is the very best thing to do. Cultivate a heart of gratitude for beauty and God's good gifts in every place you live.

Cultivate a heart of gratitude for beauty and God's good gifts in every place you live.

But the grumbling? Numbers 11 tells us that when the Israelites complained, it displeased the Lord. His anger was kindled and people died. Later the people wept again and said, "We remember the fish, which we did eat in Egypt freely; the cucumbers, and the melons, and the leeks, and the onions, and the garlick: But now our soul is dried away: there is nothing at all, beside this manna, before our eyes" (Num. 11:5-6). The anger of the Lord was kindled. Moses also was displeased.

The children of Israel in Numbers 20 complained again to their leader. "Why did you make us leave Egypt? Why are we here in this evil place? There is no water to drink, no grain, no figs and grapes. We are hungry for melons and cucumbers" (verse 5 paraphrase).

In Africa, with all the heat, dust, bugs, and germs, it was easy to become disillusioned and complain.

Why God, why did you send us to this strange place?

- Much of the water is contaminated.
- The *chai* is so sweet, with three, four, or more teaspoons of sugar.
- White bread (though it's their best and special to them) is still unhealthy white bread.
- I don't care for cooked intestines or those tiny smelly fish.
- *Ugali* is rather tasteless (but Africans love it as one of their very best foods).
- There is a scarcity of good cheeses and ice cream is so pricey.
- We would like American fruits, peaches, strawberries and apples.

Naturally, we like the foods of our homeland the best.

But what about our attitudes and grumbling? Was God pleased when the children of Israel complained? Is He pleased when I do? Thankfully, eventually, we learned to enjoy many new African foods!

May God help me to have a grateful heart, every day,
in every place, for Jesus.

Read Numbers 11 and 20

More of God's Presence

In thy presence is fulness of joy; at thy right hand there are pleasures for evermore. –Psalm 16:11

I enjoy having a word for the year, and at the beginning of 2020, I chose "Presence." Soon after I made my choice, I was amazed and blessed at how often the word popped out for me. I heard "presence" in songs, read it in the Word, and in books I read. I desire to be more aware of God's presence, and He honored my desire.

To be more joyful, we need to drink in God's presence and spend more time in His Word. While I long for the second coming of Christ, I cling to the promise of God's presence with me today. I may feel lonely, but I am never alone.

When clouds of despair obscure my sense of Your presence, You are still there, Your love is constant and abiding.

Betty Robinson said, "Lord, I need a greater sense of your presence. Give me a hunger to know you more intimately. Open my eyes to see You in the midst of struggles. May the fragrance of your presence linger with me and urge me to stay the course."

The *Life Application Study Bible* commentary on Matthew 14:30

is especially helpful in moments when God feels distant: "When you are apprehensive about the troubles around you, and doubt God's presence or ability to help, remember that He is always with you and is the only one who can really help."[1]

When clouds of despair obscure my sense of Your presence, You are still there; Your love is constant and abiding.

Words from His Word:

- "Lo, I am with you alway" (Matt. 28:20).
- "God is present in the company of the righteous" (Psa. 14:5 NIV).
- "My presence shall go with thee, and I will give thee rest" (Exod. 33:14).
- "Moses entered the Lord's presence, and his face became radiant" (Exod. 34:29-35).
- "Blessed are those . . . who walk in the light of your presence, LORD" (Psa. 89:15 NIV).
- "Thou shalt hide them in the secret of thy presence" (Psa. 31:20).

In February, Mark chose a song of the month, "Dear Shepherd of Thy People Hear." He posted these words in the church bulletin: "This song depicts a shepherd's love, care and concern for his sheep. We invoke His presence, peace, healing for wounds, openness to His Word, and growth in our walk with Him."

Lord, help me see the evidence of Your presence in small beauties: a droplet of rain, the first bright crocus in springtime, an intricate snowflake, a toddler's happy giggle, golden leaves on the trees in the fall . . .

Read Exodus 33

---

[1] *Life Application Study Bible* (Carol Stream, IL: Tyndale House Publishers, 2007), 1573.

A Gracious
Mother-in-Law

*Every wise woman buildeth her house: but the foolish
plu_cketh it down with her hands.* –Proverbs 14:1

I appreciated advice from my friend who has much more experience in being a mother-in-law than I do. She shared:

The truth is, in so many things, I must know that I don't
have what it takes—it is only as the life of God flows into
my heart and fills those empty broken places that I can be a
truly gracious mother-in-law. I have two daughters-in-law
and three sons-in-law. I love them all dearly. Each of them
has blessed me in their own unique way. We all help with
meals when we get together. I appreciate that. Sometimes
the men grill the meat. Working together makes it easier for
everyone.

One of my daughters-in-law took more effort to develop a
close relationship with me. I have learned to love and appreciate her. I like to babysit, but my daughters and daughters-in-law don't take advantage of that, which I also appreciate. These
last weeks during the "Stay-at-home" order, I take care of their
children when they need to get groceries because they don't
want to take the children. They often pick up things for me
then, which helps us both.

When our sons and daughters get married, it is important

we recognize that they are now a new family. It's okay if the new wife, our daughter-in-law, does things differently than we did, even if our way feels better. Often, it's better not to give advice unless they ask. We need to express appreciation to them.

"When our sons and daughters get married, it is important we recognize that they are now a new family."

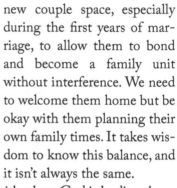

It is important to give the new couple space, especially during the first years of marriage, to allow them to bond and become a family unit without interference. We need to welcome them home but be okay with them planning their own family times. It takes wisdom to know this balance, and it isn't always the same.

It's important to be okay with where God is leading them, and to visit them if they live in a different community.

Lord, help me to recognize and accept wisdom when it is offered.

Read Psalms 127 and 128

Show Kindness

K indness. The word jumped out at me in these three different verses recently during morning time with God.

- "And David said, is there yet any that is left of the house of Saul, that I may show him kindness for Jonathan's sake?" (2 Sam. 9:1).
- "Blessed is the one who is kind to the needy" (Prov. 14:21 NIV).
- "May the LORD show you kindness and faithfulness" (2 Sam. 15:20 NIV).

How can I show kindness in ordinary days as I go about my daily duties, as I tend the greenhouse? I ask God, and He gives ideas.

We enjoy inviting friends over and summertime is perfect for outdoor entertaining. On one Sunday evening, two families came over for a hotdog roast. One lady brought buns and drinks, and the other brought mini-cheesecakes. I did not have time to fix fancy foods. Her cheesecakes were special. The children tried to catch the bullfrogs in the water-pond. They enjoyed watching the goldfish, even though one li'l miss accidentally slid into the water. Mark played corn hole with lively youngsters.

> *Kindness is like a pebble thrown on the water; the ripples grow and widen, spreading on and on.*

Later, my friend commented, "Thanks for your hospitality. You inspired us to invite people to our backyard for a simple supper too."

A young lady came to the greenhouse. She stayed awhile to chat. Her visit blessed me, and I hope my words were an encouragement. Taking time to talk with friends is kind. Listening is kindness.

Do I have open hands to share, even simple things like bread, plants, and fresh garden lettuce?

I came indoors on a busy day and there on my table was a fresh loaf of sourdough bread. A slice with butter and honey was a refreshing afternoon snack, thanks to my kind neighbor.

Our deacon's objective for Sunday's message was to encourage us to read and study more in God's Word. Would we grow more kind and loving if we were to spend more time with the life-giving and life-changing Word of God?

Will I give encouraging kind words? Will I let the bearer of the Word know I appreciated the message, and that I had heard numerous people say the same?

Picking up the phone to express appreciation or writing a note does not take long.

Our family operates a small greenhouse business. I hope our customers can see a face of love and kindness in me. A friend from church came to shop; later she gave me a simple yellow Post-it note. The message cheered me: "You have a beautiful greenhouse. We love coming there. Thank you for the pretty plants you gifted my daughter. She says you are her grandma and wishes you were her mom." I valued that note.

Kindness is like a pebble thrown on the water; the ripples grow and widen, spreading on and on.

Lord, help me to show kindness to others every day.
Inspire me to share simple things, a listening ear,
encouraging words . . .

Read Ephesians 4:25-32

In the Night Watches

*When I remember thee upon my bed, and meditate
on thee in the night watches.* –Psalm 63:6

I love when I wake up at night and a gospel song is running through my mind. What will I do when I awaken with my mind filled with concerns and care?

My mind will be filled. What to fill it with is my choice. I want to make it a habit to think and talk more with Jesus. I can either dwell on the negative messages that come my way or I can choose to fill my mind with God's Word and edifying literature each day. I can choose to think on that which is true, good, lovely, pure, honorable, excellent, and admirable.

- "I lie down and sleep; I wake again, because the LORD sustains me" (Psa. 3:5 NIV).
- "Stand in awe, and sin not: commune with your own heart upon your bed, and be still. I will both lay me down in peace, and sleep; for thou, LORD, only makest me dwell in safety" (Psa. 4:4, 8).
- "Remember God, meditate on Him in the night watches" (Psa. 63:6).
- "Let the saints be joyful in glory: let them sing aloud upon their beds" (Psa. 149:5).

I am challenged with the words of Jim Stump: "Jesus is the first person I talk to when I wake up in the morning, and the last person I talk to when I lay down at night."[2]

When I cannot fall asleep, I have learned that it is a great idea to talk to Jesus. I pray for our family and friends when sleep eludes me. If I still cannot fall asleep after prayer, it may be good for me to get up and read the Word of God, chapter after chapter filling my heart and mind with truth.

What will I do when I awaken with my mind filled with concerns and care?

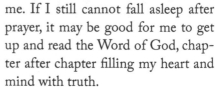

A friend shared a creative way to pray when sleeplessness assaults her. She prays as far as she can get through the alphabet, praying for someone whose name starts with each letter: "A, I am praying for Adam, Ann, Anna. B, my cousin Barbara, Betty, Bobby. C, Carrisa, Carrie, Cory. D, David . . ."

Will Jesus be the last one I speak with at night and the first I communicate with in the morning and whenever I awake in between?

Jesus, help me remember You each night as I fall asleep
and each morning as I wake to a new day,
and during my night watches.

Read Colossians 1:1-17

---

[2]Jim Stump, *The Power of One-On-One* (Grand Rapids: Baker Books, 2014), 97.

Do Not Be Afraid

That thy trust may be in the Lord. –Proverbs 22:19

Warm sunshine kisses the earth. The fields and yards are turning a refreshing green. Crocuses add bright splashes of color. The curly green rhubarb leaves are pushing out of the soil. All nature sings the praises of our wonderful Jesus!

It's amazing how fast plants grow in a warm sunny greenhouse. The pansies are blooming. Their cheery faces brighten spaces. Plants in a greenhouse soak up water and shoot out growth on bright days.

This morning I read a thought I am pondering: kindness makes friends. God gives ideas on ways to show kindness in church and other places this season.

Jesus, my Jesus, satisfies and renews.

Kindness has blessed and brightened my days so often:

- A loaf of Italian bread dough, still rising, handed to me over the porch gate. What can rival fresh homemade bread?
- A son washing dishes without me asking; Mark drying them and sweeping the floor.
- Friends and daughters called; connections are special.
- Two ladies came to the greenhouse to discuss plants for weddings. One gave me a dozen farm-fresh eggs.
- Two church friends and I sat outside chatting, trying to maintain a social distance of six feet. I need friends; I don't

want to go through life or through COVID alone. However, I do want to be careful to not spread germs.

Through all these things, Psalm 103 says to remember benefits:

- Jesus forgives all our iniquities.
- He heals all our diseases, redeems us from destruction.
- He crowns us with loving kindness and tender mercies.

Jesus, my Jesus, satisfies and renews.

I wonder what will happen yet with COVID. It seems the world is spinning crazily out of control with this pandemic. My son won't be out of a job, as he works in the emergency room in Canton, Ohio. I pray for his safety.

Mark's music classes are canceled. He has more time at home. Our church has canceled the last two Sundays. I wonder what will happen next?

We are surprised by events, but nothing is a surprise to our Father. I want to trust and not be afraid. I want to hold on to the promises of the Word of God.

In a world of turmoil and confusion, thank You Jesus that
you are my Rock and Strength.

Read Psalm 103

One May Day in Kenya

Charge them that are rich in this world, that they be not highminded, nor trust in uncertain riches, but in the living God, who giveth us richly all things to enjoy.
−1 Timothy 6:17

O ne sunny day, Mark and I drove down a back bumpy road. We picked up our widow friend, Margaret, who was delighted to go along to visit Jo, a woman she cared about, who lived in abject poverty. We took a box of groceries for her. Jo always expressed heartfelt gratitude when we brought her food.

Margaret and Jo were praising the Lord for the good things in their lives. Jo can hardly walk; she creeps around with a walker. She was thanking God for a woman who lives with her and does her cooking.

In contrast, as I sat in Jo's mud hut, I did not feel very grateful. I was appalled at the many ants crawling over the floors and up the walls. These walls were pockmarked with insect holes. The chickens came in and out; they pooped on the floor. The hut smelled like fowls. I smelled other things too . . . body odor and urine.

To top it off, I felt like I was slowly cooking in the heat of the day.

The chairs and sofa consisted of only hard wooden frames. There were no soft cushions for comfort. There were so many needs. We could never meet them all. But Jo was grateful that day in her mud hut. This was her culture. This was her home.

Relating to folks in poverty in foreign lands is difficult. We should not make them dependent on us by providing all the solutions to what we perceive as their lack. But surely we can show love.

One day we gifted Jo foam cushions for her sofa. Afterward, we prayed, read the Word, and sang with her.

In contrast to many other lands, each one of us lives in a mansion.

Are we grateful for where we live? In contrast to many other lands, each one of us lives in a mansion.

A young African man saw a picture of my daughter's house. He wondered how many people lived there. He thought it was big enough for twenty people.

If you have riches, you carry a great responsibility. Thank the Lord for the gifts He gives you, share with others, be generous. *Trust Him*, not your wealth. No matter how much you possess or how much money you make, you have nothing if you don't have a vital relationship with Christ.

True value is not in material possessions, but in a right relationship with Jesus Christ.

Lord, help us keep our focus on You,
not on material possessions.

Read 1 Timothy 6

Together
Fifty Years

And the LORD God said, It is not good that the man should be alone; I will make him a help meet for him.
–Genesis 2:18

Often a couple marries when they are in the prime of life. They are young. Beautiful. Strong. Energetic. Hopeful. Full of dreams.

When vows are spoken, one cannot know everything life will hold. Will there be health or illness? Will there be prosperity or adversity? The promise to love and to cherish each other throughout all of life is binding, breathtaking, and beautiful.

Here's the testimony of my friend Irene:

We've had fifty years of life together, and my husband becomes a better partner every day. There are so many little things he does for me without complaint. He is noted for having big strong hands. Those hands bless me constantly. Due to health issues, he always ties my shoes. As we get older, we are here for one another. I have to remember the things he forgets, and he remembers the things I forget.

He does all the book work in our home. He always has. He knows where our money comes from and goes. I learned to trust him completely with all our finances.

We have had many things to work on through life. With

the grace of God, we are still trying to stay on top. A crucial part in our marriage for me was to learn to trust my husband and not run ahead of him. He is not a man of many words. I had to learn to let him lead. Things do fall in place and work out for us.

When we were a dating couple so many years ago, we practiced a hands-off policy. That was a blessing for us.

Sometimes I wonder if I really love him enough? If he is gone for a few days, I wonder how I could do without him. Yes, I do love him. Sometimes I fail to tell him how much I love him.

"Marriage is a process of learning to live in love, communication, care and kindness."

Marriage is a process of learning to live in love, communication, care and kindness.

I personally experience Jesus every day when I walk with Him by reading His Word, prayer, and fellowship with Christians. Jesus is the true guide for my life. Then trusting my husband and being in submission helps me be a blessing to my children and grandchildren.

Despite all the bumps in the road we have come through fifty years of marriage. We praise the Lord for His many blessings.

Lord, thank You for Your gift of marriage.

Read Ephesians 5:21-33

Heart Longings

And the peace of God, which passeth all understanding,
shall keep your hearts and minds through Christ Jesus. –
Philippians 4:7

We long for beautiful and well-behaved children. We long for our children to grow up to live for Jesus. The Word of God tells us of three things that will help our children to be wise:

- "The rod and reproof give wisdom" (Prov. 29:15).
- "Correct thy son, and he shall give thee rest; yea, he shall give delight unto thy soul" (Prov. 29:17).
- "And that from a child thou hast known the holy scriptures, which are able to make thee wise unto salvation through faith which is in Christ Jesus" (2 Tim. 3:15).

These scriptures tell us it pays to take time to teach obedience and manners. Children will not wait to be naughty when you have time to discipline. Without teaching, they will act badly when you are busy.

Even though your days are filled with duties, it is worthwhile to fill children's minds with the Word of God. Little tots can easily memorize many verses before they are old enough to go to school. Write verses on poster boards. Put them on the wall where you can see them. Review them when you eat lunch. Read those verses every day. Put another paper by their bed and make reviewing a bedtime ritual. When you go away with the children, make it fun to recite verses while driving.

Pray for your children. Trace their hand on a stiff piece of paper and write their name on it. Tell them what you are going to pray; ask them for ideas. Jot them down and hang it on the wall by their bed. When you tuck them in, linger; take time to chat. Bedtime is an excellent time to hear their heart. I remember a small son expressing fear about the first day of school coming up. Listening and praying is so important.

> *We long for our children to grow up to live for Jesus.*

Love and enjoy your children. Take time to read. Don't always be working. At one time it felt like I would forever have a small one on my skirts. Today my children are grown. I don't regret the countless books and stories I read to them and the verses, songs, and prayers we learned, praised, and prayed together. Now I have grandchildren to love. The cycles of life are amazing, perplexing, and precious.

When adult children have struggles, the best thing to do is spend time in prayer, interceding for them. God can work in ways we cannot.

God loves each of us, wherever we are in life. He understands the work and cares of motherhood. He knows our hearts long for sons and daughters who love and serve Him.

Lord, You understand my mother heart.
I cast the cares of my children on You.

Read Proverbs 29:15-27

An Hour for Beauty

But let it be the hidden man of the heart, in that which is not corruptible, even the ornament of a meek and quiet spirit, which is in the sight of God of great price. –1 Peter 3:4

How can I be beautiful? What am I willing to do to enhance beauty?

I once read of a survey where women who reported spending nearly an hour on their looks daily said it made them feel better about themselves. I also read that the average American woman spends $18,000 on make-up during her life. This comes to $15.45 a month for products to beautify herself.

What can my daughter with small children do for beauty? Posting verses and inspirational thoughts on the wall can help direct her mind to Jesus. She cannot spend an hour a day on looks. Small children want to be in the bathroom whenever mom is there. One day when she told her son to wait, he said, "I will lose some teeth if I cannot get in the bathroom right now."

Mothers, and all women, need to spend time with Jesus, the One who gives us true and lasting beauty. Be intentional to work time with God into your daily schedule.

In the morning, I often feel slightly grumpy and tired. But when I rise, I spend time reading the Word in our sunroom among beautiful plants while drinking coffee. I jot in my notebook thoughts that inspire me from the Word and I pray. God gives me an attitude adjustment.

There are blessings in every time of life. I love my quiet times with God in the morning.

I do believe each of us can make time for God if we really want to. If not in the morning, try afternoons when the children nap. If they cannot nap, they can learn to be quiet somewhere while mother reads and prays.

Mothers, and all women, need to spend time with Jesus, the One who gives us true and lasting beauty.

Take women of faith as your example, not fashion models. No amount of finery can substitute for a gracious and godly character.

I choose beauty by spending time with God. I choose beauty by cultivating a grateful heart.

Will I spend a daily hour to nurture my soul?

Most of all, Jesus, I want Your beauty to be seen in me.

Read Psalm 1 and Psalm 5

What If?

Ye are of God, little children, and have overcome them:
because greater is he that is in you, than he
that is in the world. –1 John 4:4

The day's class at youth Bible School in Nakuru was from Proverbs 31. I asked the girls to share good things from the chapter that God wants for women. I was happy the African girls were talking more. Toward the end of class, one of the girls asked, "What are we to do if our husband beats us?"

We had a good discussion. This is truly difficult in a culture where wife-beating is expected. Sons learn from their father's example. Men say, "I beat my wife to discipline her." What can a woman do? One thing is for sure—it is not easy, but you can ask God to help you be kind, respectful, and loving. Determine with God's help to give good for evil.

> *Thankfully, the power of God gives us victory over sin, and God's power is stronger than Satan.*
>
>

I believe God can help Christians to do much better than wife-beating. But cultural norms die hard. It has even been said that if a man has never beaten his wife when she is alive, he should beat her corpse after she dies.

I asked the girls what they want in a husband? The men's teacher asked the men what they want in a wife. I compiled what both classes shared, then we exchanged notes. They enjoyed that very much.

Six P's was the title of another class. The P's represented parents, pastors, prayer, purity, phones, and pornography.

On pornography, John Regier says:

> Much of pornography comes infused with the power of demonic spirits which infiltrate and become an indwelling ongoing part of those who have given themselves to that kind of involvement. A 2002 Barna survey revealed that millions of Christians are involved in gambling and pornography on a regular basis! As we let that fact sink in, we realize what is happening to the church in America.[3]

Pornography will turn your heart from God. It will cause problems and dissatisfaction when married. Another frightening truth of pornography is that it opens a heart to demonic spirits. Thankfully, the power of God gives us victory over sin, and God's power is stronger than Satan.

Back to the question, "What if he beats me?"

Whatever you experience, with God, you can return good for evil.

Lord, help us to do as You tell us to do.
Help us return good for evil.

Read Ephesians 5:22-33

---

[3] As cited by Evelyn Miller, *Feminine Beauty* (Biblical Mennonite Alliance, 2016), 73.

Open Gates

Blessed are they that do his commandments, that they may
have right to the tree of life, and may enter in through the
gates into the city. –Revelation 22:14

An open gate speaks of warmth and welcome. There is nothing like someone we love standing there with a smile, beckoning us to come in.

I never understood much about walls and gates until I lived in Africa. I was accustomed to wide open spaces and country places. I felt hemmed in with high walls and thick hedges full of thorns when we moved to the city of Kisumu. I could not see over the walls. But when I stood at a certain spot, there was a lovely distant view of hazy mountains.

Our yard had an entrance gate. The compound had a big solid main gate. The gateman decided who was allowed to enter. It was strange to always have to go in and out of gates.

In Africa, walls and gates are common. Most people with any wealth value the safety of walls and gates, which afford privacy and protection from thieves and robbers and a shield against poverty-stricken beggars. The walls and gates gave a measure of quietness and security in the city.

Mark and I went on morning walks. The gateman would open the gate so we could go out. On our way back one morning, we picked up some rocks on the stony lane. I wanted them for my flower beds, to protect plants from our dog. When the gateman opened the gate on our return, he was shocked to see rocks in our hands. We explained to him the purpose for the rocks. In Kenya, rocks in the hand mean hatred and trouble. People grab rocks to stone a thief or someone who has raised their anger.

Although there were walls and gates, thieves still entered. One night thieves somehow climbed over the neighbor's wall into their yard. The Asian couple struggled with fear. After that night, they had sharp, cutting razor wire installed in silver coils along their walls and above their gates.

"Safety is of the LORD."

Robberies occurred in mission houses. Thieves came into a dark house while a couple slept. They snuck all through the house, even the bedroom. They stole many things. This happened more than once. It is easy to become fearful in a foreign land.

God often brought Proverbs 21:31b to my mind: "Safety is of the LORD." In the midst of robberies and troubles, can we believe prayer to be our mainstay, and God our best security?

You, O Father, are my security and sure victory.

Read Revelation 21

Walls and Gates

And the gates of it shall not be shut at all by day: for there shall be no night there. –Revelation 21:25

In some countries, when walls are constructed, broken shards of glass are stuck in place along the top of the wet cement of the new wall. Sharp razor wire may be installed too. People install security cameras so in the morning they can see if anyone was in their compound at night. Motels and businesses have their own high walls and guarded gates.

My Kenyan friends were amazed when I told them that our house in America has no walls or gates. They could not understand it.

I had the opportunity to befriend some schoolgirls who lived in a nearby slum. The gateman informed me when the girls arrived. We met in a shelter outside the gate. We sang. I shared Bible stories and they learned verses. They were intrigued with my white skin and liked to touch my hair. One day, I invited them into our house for a drink. They were thrilled to come in through our open gate and open door. In their eyes, our mission house was a mansion, and the green grass in the yard was heavenly. We sat in our yard to look at Bible picture cards and to read a Bible story.

Heaven is a home where no sin can enter, the gates are open, and there is no night.

When we lived in Ng'iya, our yard did not have high walls. There was a big main gate to the compound where African families and our family lived. The front gate was not locked or guarded during the day. Every night, the yard man, Solomon, dutifully locked the gate.

Our sons and visiting friends came home late one night. They had asked Solomon to leave the gate unlocked, but when they got to the front gate, it was barred. They could have tooted the horn, calling for Solomon. Instead, they left the van outside the gate and easily climbed over the wall. They were home.

We read that heaven is a city with walls and gates. The gates are always standing open. Our Father is waiting to welcome us home. Do I live with anticipation for my heavenly home?

Heaven is a home where no sin can enter, the gates are open, and there is no night. What a wonderful day when I get home to be with Jesus forever. Wherever we go, I look forward to going home.

Lord, thank You for the assurance that after
this life I will be with You forever.

Read John 10

Look Your Child in the Eye

Be thou diligent to know the state of thy flocks, and look well to thy herds. –Proverbs 27:23

For many years now my son has raised and sold Golden Retrievers. His operation has grown big enough that an inspector stopped in and gave guidelines that apply to raising dogs in Ohio. There are laws in place to protect those doggies.

He found out:

- Each pen has to have a toy or bone for their enrichment.
- Shade must be provided on outdoor runs.
- A barrier is required between pens to provide privacy for every dog.
- Dogs must have an annual physical.
- My son gets a background check. No criminal should raise dogs.
- A female is only allowed to have eight litters.

Some couples choose to have a dog rather than to have a child. I have been amazed at customers who kiss the puppy and exclaim delightedly over puppy breath and puppy kisses.

My widowed neighbor has a house dog. She heard that people with pets should be careful about how much they are on their electronic devices. She also said owners should take time to look their dog in the eye. I imagine talking to dogs is also important. Dogs are nicer to live with when trained to obey too.

Hello mothers! If dogs are important . . . your children are even more so. I encourage you to get off your phone (at least use moderation) and care for your dear little ones. Look them in the eye. What will they remember about you?

Accept and embrace the work of mothering given to you by God.

Is being on the phone how we want to be remembered?

Rather than looking out so carefully for your pooch, or holding your phone so often, take time with God, with children, and with friends. In this digital age, it is so easy to neglect and ignore those we live with and connect instead with myriad friends who live elsewhere.

Love your family well. Remember, if you have children, they are your flock. What are you doing to nurture their souls, to encourage them, to show them love and acceptance? Don't neglect your children. Accept and embrace the work of mothering given to you by God.

Don't let the majority of your time be spent with your pets or on your phone. Look your daughter or son in the eye, hold your child or children, read many stories together, and say "I love you" often.

Help me Jesus, to be less distracted and
fully present with my children.

Read Isaiah 40:1-18

This Mother-in-Law Thing

Therefore all things whatsoever ye would that men should do to you, do ye even so to them; for this is the law and the prophets. –Matthew 7:12

I enjoy brainstorming with my daughters about many things. They shared what they appreciate about their mothers-in-law. We appreciate it when:

- She offers to do my laundry after a baby or when she sees I am overwhelmed.
- She makes specific offers, which is nice! (Vs. vague "let me know if you need help.")
- She is a fantastic babysitter. It's such a blessing how she genuinely loves our children.
- Her eyes are open for ways I need help.
- I appreciated when she taught our oldest son kindergarten.
- She expresses her enjoyment of being around my children.
- She's truly happy to spend time with them and babysit them.
- She invites us for meals.

Be generous in expressing appreciation for everything your mother-in-law does for you.

- She's just herself, confident in who God made her to be.
- She does well in expressing her appreciation for things she likes or admires about me.
- I'm also glad if she is honest if it doesn't work to babysit. I want her to be able to say no.
- She enjoys and accepts our family members. That is one of the biggest gifts you can give.

Years ago, Mark's parents took time to come help if I had a busy day of canning. Meals at their house were special. His mother was an awesome cook. They loved when we came over in the evening. It blessed them when we sang. Grandpa gave out M&Ms. Their grandsons loved that. They were not supposed to beg, but at times they gave creative hints.

Mothers-in-law say:

- I love to babysit. Grandchildren are just special. Consideration needs to be used with the age of the grandma and how many grandchildren are nearby.
- I like to be enjoyed as a person, not just for my babysitting.

Be generous in expressing appreciation for everything your mother-in-law does for you.

Bless her on Mother's Day and throughout the year with kind words. Gifts are not mandatory, but meaningful, sincere words, spoken or on a card, should not be neglected.

Mothers-in-law love to be invited over for meals and most of them enjoy going out to eat.

My son came in carrying a bright cheery Poinsettia for me before Christmas. That was a sweet expression of appreciation for babysitting.

Through all the changes in life, I need Your
constant love and presence, Lord.

Read 1 Peter 3

Choose Love

Choose you this day whom ye will serve . . . but as for me and my house, we will serve the Lord. –Joshua 24:15

J ohn 12 contains the story of Mary and Judas. The house was filled with the fragrance of Mary's love as she knelt and anointed the feet of Jesus with pricey perfume. She chose to show her extravagant love by giving her best. Mary delighted in spending time with Jesus. Mary's heart was a pure heart of love.

Judas, in contrast, chose a black heart. He found fault with Mary's gift of love. He did not care for the poor, though he complained that the spikenard could have been sold to help the poor (John 12:5). Judas was a thief. Why was he in charge of the disciples' money? He often dipped into the bag for his own purposes. He was smooth and suave. Yet Jesus knew what Judas was doing, even if his thievery was hidden from the other men. Judas was gifted, yet, despite being one of the twelve, he was a real hypocrite.

Jesus loved His disciples unto the end.

Jesus is all-knowing. Did Jesus do anything to expose or reprimand Judas? Did the other eleven disciples know? If they did, it seems they would not have allowed him to be the treasurer.

God may not immediately stop a person when they choose sin. Yet what a person deserves will come. A lying character opens the door to Satan's influence. Judas was opening the door of his heart

more and more to Satan. In the end, Judas believed the fatal black
lie from Satan that life was not worth living.

Jesus loved His disciples unto the end. Jesus loved Judas.

My heart is consoled with the fact that Jesus loves me.

Jesus loves each one of us, and He told us to love each other as
He loves us.

Do I show love to a person who is struggling with sin?

Do I show love when someone acts in a way that I think is
immature?

Am I full of love and kindness, or criticism and condemna-
tion?

Am I willing to live with nothing to hide?

How will I show my love for my Lord?

Oh Jesus, love through me.

Read John 12

Calm
Commitment

I n life we need to care for each other. Kindness is sunshine to our days. In marriage, we surely need a lot of kindness.

Mark had been forgetting numerous things. He forgot his checkbook when he went away. He forgot to stop and buy some things I requested. One day, he even forgot he was supposed to be on a tour bus. At our age, when we do such things, we hope we aren't showing early signs of mind deterioration.

I really do need to be patient and kind, because I forget too.

One day I drove to Hillcrest Orchard for lettuce. I told Mark I would take the checks along to the bank. I went to the orchard first and stuck the checks in the glove compartment. I never ever once thought again about the checks until late afternoon, when Mark asked me about it.

Bless his dear, kind heart. He did not say one unkind word. I am sure my forgetfulness was annoying. I apologized and remarked that I could take care of the banking on Monday.

I was rather taken aback when a newly-married lady asked me if marriage keeps getting better and better. "That's a personal question," I responded. "I have not found marriage to just slide along into more love and goodness. It takes commitment, determination, and God's help to live and grow in love."

One day, I was helping Mark restock bookracks for Lantern Books. I also wanted to shop. He finished the rack before I finished shopping. He kindly told me to take my time. He was patient. That blessed my heart and brightened the day.

Lois Tverberg, in *Walking in the Dust of Rabbi Jesus*, relates how she was born last of seven. "The love I saw between my parents was not a newlywed passion but a calm commitment to travel through life's highs and lows together. Our lives were stably anchored in a loving family. By weathering life's storms together year after year, they embodied God's *hesed* (steadfast, rock-solid faithfulness that endures to eternity)."[4]

> *"It takes commitment, determination, and God's help to live and grow in love."*

Newlywed passion is sweet in its season. I am grateful for the fruit of faithful love and commitment that grows in love and kindness, lasting through the years.

*Lord, may our marriage have the fruits of
faithful love, kindness, and commitment.*

Read 1 Peter 3

---

[4] Lois Tverberg, *Walking in the Dust of Rabbi Jesus* (Grand Rapids: Zondervan, 2012), 50.

Support Him

Glorify God in your body, and in your spirit,
which are God's. –1 Corinthians 6:20

Each of us is called to support our husbands. It is good to study your own husband and learn how to please him. Showing support can mean:

- To agree with
- To approve
- To give help or assistance
- To promote his interest
- To keep from fainting, yielding, or losing courage.

Support him in your own unique marriage. For some ladies that means a lot of travel; for others it means staying home most of the time. It may mean being willing to spend years in a foreign land. Supporting involves adapting to his work, whether it is teaching, preaching, medical professions, farming, or a day worker. First Peter 3 encourages us to adapt—to submit to your own husband and accept his authority.

> *A woman is the spirit of the home, the light in the window.*

A woman is the spirit of the home, the light in the window. How is my light? What kind of spirit am I manifesting in my home? First Peter 3:4 reminds us that it is precious in God's sight when a woman has a gentle and quiet spirit. Verse five tells us this is possible when we trust God.

Some friends told me how they support and honor their husbands:

"Every wife needs to cry out to God for wisdom on how to honor her husband. I firmly believe that if a woman is truly seeking God's face, He will give her divine wisdom in any situation. Advice from others has its place, but if she's not first seeking it from God, it won't do much good."

"Do I choose to do what he wants, even when he allows me to choose otherwise? Recently he said it's up to me when I had the chance to make a spur-of-the-moment trip to see my sister and her new baby. I wanted to go, so I thought about it and said, 'I'll go.' Had I decided too quickly? I hadn't prayed about it. When I texted him what I'd decided, he texted back, 'I wish you wouldn't.' I was willing to honor him (I'm not always so quick to be willing). I gave up the trip and was relieved."

"I've learned as a farmer's wife that cheerful flexibility is a blessing to both of us. Grumbling (even in my heart) causes conflict. He doesn't choose delays. My attitude makes the day pleasant or unpleasant. I want to do better in dropping what I've planned and going with him. He loves when I go [with him]."

God's approval matters. My husband's approval matters too. I will answer to God for my response to my husband. Is God pleased with me?

Help me, Father, to choose daily to be true
to You and to my husband.

Read 1 Corinthians 7

Women's Fears

Casting all your care upon him; for he careth for you.
–1 Peter 5:7

Two African women confided that they were afraid at night. They feared evil men might come and break through the wall of their mud hut, steal their things, or worse yet, abuse them.

A widow told me that she and her granddaughter go in their hut in the evening while it is still daylight. They lock up everything tight in hopes of being safe. They said they cannot even let laundry and household things outside when they go away, or someone might take their belongings. The chickens are brought into the hut for safekeeping. If there is a calf, it is brought in as well.

> *Whenever worries come to bother us, we have the privilege to pray again.*

Does God sleep? The One who watches over us will never slumber or sleep. I encouraged the woman to pray every night, asking God to watch over them. God is much stronger than all the evil men.

We pray for our children. Still we are tempted to worry that they could have an accident, grow cold toward God, or make unwise choices. What can be done to alleviate our fears?

Whenever worries come to bother us, we have the privilege to pray again.

Here are weapons against worry:

- Read the Word every morning; commit your day and your family to God.
- Write down prayers and give concerns to God.
- Hold on to the promises in God's Word. Pray the promises.
- Record answers to prayers.
- Write verses on a file card and post them on your wall where you see them often.
- Share your fears with your husband or a trusted friend. We are not meant to travel alone on the road of life.
- Ask a friend to pray for you and with you.
- Share with a friend the prayers God has answered.

Hold on to the many wonderful promises in the Word of God.

"Cast thy burden upon the Lord, and he shall sustain thee; he shall never suffer the righteous to be moved" (Psalm 55:22).

"Fear thou not; for I am with thee: be not dismayed; for I am thy God: I will strengthen thee; yea, I will help thee; yea, I will uphold thee with the right hand of my righteousness" (Isaiah 41:10).

God, I hold on to Your presence and power. Thank You that You are much greater than all my fears.

Read Psalm 121

Grateful or Not

Blessed be the Lord, who daily loadeth us with benefits,
*even the God of our salvation. Selah. –*Psalm 68:19

Luke is the only one who recorded the story of the ten lepers. These sick men had to leave their homes and loved ones so the disease would not spread. They became outcasts from family and society. No one wanted to touch them or be near them. One wonderful day, they saw Jesus. "Jesus, Master, have mercy on us," they cried out. Jesus had mercy on those men. They were healed. What a transformation! The opportunity for a life full of purpose with family and community was restored. Imagine those nine lepers racing to the priest, then running home to their families.

Our hearts should overflow with gratefulness for the gift of Jesus, for His healing, and His love.

Of the ten, one lone man came back to Jesus. He glorified God and fell on his face at Jesus's feet, giving Him thanks. Why did they not all express gratitude to the Master?

If the lepers in this biblical account are a fair representation of humanity, then we have a 90% rate of ingratitude. Nine out of ten failed the gratitude test. The grateful one was a despised Samaritan. The grateful man was from what the Jews considered an inferior race.

One day at church in Kenya, there was a lady whose fingers were stubs. Her eyes were watery and looked strange. I had never seen her before. Could she actually have leprosy? If so, I was shocked. She shook hands with many people. I felt fearful of her germs. At home that afternoon, we researched leprosy. I was relieved to learn that leprosy is not spread by casual contact. Today there is treatment for lepers, but for people stuck in poverty, many cannot afford proper medical care. They may not be willing to travel far from home.

We may not have leprosy, but sin is a leprosy that defiles us and affects those around us. Jesus came to destroy the curse of sin. Just as He healed the lepers, He heals and helps all who come to Him. Our hearts should overflow with gratefulness for the gift of Jesus, for His healing, and His love.

Do I come to God with a grateful heart? It is possible to receive God's great gifts with an ungrateful spirit. God does not demand that we thank Him, but He is pleased when we do.

Choose gratitude to God, regardless of your circumstances.

Help me to have a grateful heart, my Father God,
regardless of my circumstances.

Read Luke 17:11-19

Guidance and Protection

*My voice shalt thou hear in the morning, O Lord; in the
morning will I direct my prayer unto thee, and will look up.*
–Psalm 5:3

"Lord, show me what you want me to do today," I prayed
on a Monday morning. Then I felt prompted to visit
Mary. Her niece was very ill and had come to Mary's
house to live out her remaining days. HIV ravages a body and the
suffering is horrible; it lingers until the sufferer gasps for air and
their body just wastes away.

I bought groceries for Mary at the market and drove to her
house. The sick lady was lying on an old sofa, breathing heavily.
I read scriptures that day and prayed for the desperately-ill niece.

My friend Sharon came with me to Mary's to interpret. We
talked of many things in Mary's well-swept, tidy hut. When I left,
I wondered how many days the young lady had left.

Early the next morning, Mary hired a *pikipiki* (motorcycle) to
come to our house to tell us her niece had died.

I was grateful I had gone to Mary's house the day before. I knew
God led me. Mary felt her niece was ready to die. Prayers rested
her heart.

Powers of Darkness
Witch doctors cast spells on people. The first time we looked at our

rental house, I saw a sign for a witch doctor along the main road. Satan was not happy that we moved out there.

The last few months, we had some especially difficult times in the church and in our home. Satan was trying to destroy and attack us. It affected my sleep. It seemed that every breath at night needed to be a gasping prayer, a cry to God to protect and sustain those I loved so much. Through it all, God WAS THERE.

Were all the fatigue, the problems, illnesses, and adjustments worth our time? Was the loneliness for family who were ten thousand miles away worth it? What is the worth of a soul?

Through it all, God WAS THERE.

Africa is full of so many crying needs. We saw hungry people. We saw sick people. We saw huge tumors that stuck out at odd places. We saw crippled people who could not walk dragging themselves along on the ground. We saw hands reaching out for help and desperate, pleading eyes. We often gave a few coins, but we could not help everyone. God helped us minister. Sometimes my heart felt weary and worn and I would turn away.

Missionaries are on the front lines of battle. Their families need our fervent prayers. Prayer is powerful. Prayer is something we can do for those we love. Pray, and let your friends on the mission field know that you are praying.

*I cast my cares on You, Jesus, believing in Your love
and goodness through the rough roads in life.*

Read Psalm 3

When Danger Threatens

*Behold, I send an Angel before thee, to keep thee
in the way, and to bring thee into the place
which I have prepared.* –Exodus 23:20

On the Roads

Africans drive wildly. There are few stop signs and countless huge
speed bumps to help traffic flow. At intersections, traffic merges
from all directions. One must drive defensively. There are drivers
without licenses and countless motorcycles. Brake failures on old
semi-trucks cause horrible accidents. Our sons worked for Agape
Ministries in Kenya delivering food parcels; they traveled the roads.
Cattle are guarded by children and are loose and roaming. Once
they nearly hit a cow. I prayed for my sons and was not consumed
by worry, though I was relieved whenever they rolled safely through
our gate.

Protection from Evil Men

God was with us there and answered prayers the day a riot broke
out at church. Africans can be worked into a frenzy and form a
mob. But those against us that day were not joined by many others.
Vehicles were not destroyed; we were unharmed.

Africa is wild. Thieves are caught and burned. Rocks are thrown.

Protection in the Night

God went with us when we moved. At night we knelt and prayed for protection. We frequently heard loud, drunken men on the road. During wakes, music vibrated through the night. God was awake.

Malaria

Malaria includes high fevers and leaves a person weak and depressed. One night when our son was sick with malaria I heard him in the kitchen. He nearly fainted. I clung to him and somehow got him down on the cold cement floor. I worried if my sons would ever be hale and hearty again. God answered prayers for healing.

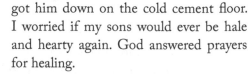

I walked country roads and paths alone, but not alone, for God was with me.

Serpents

I fear snakes. Black mambas, green mambas, puff adders, and spitting cobras are venomous African varieties. I saw one small snake on the sidewalk in the city compound. When we moved to the African interior, I continued to pray for protection. Thankfully, I never saw a big snake in our fenced yard. A large black mamba was killed outside the main gate. One day we found a small snake in our bathroom. Driving along the road in the mission van, I spotted a huge snake with its head high. Involuntarily, I jerked away from the window.

A man was herding cattle and stepped on a snake. He could not get help in time. Hospitals did not always have the anti-venom available.

I walked country roads and paths alone, but not alone, for God was with me.

Africa may be dangerous, but if God calls you, go.

Lord, thank You for the promise that Your angels encamp around those who fear You.

Read Psalm 34

Many Prayers in Kenya

He shall call upon me, and I will answer him: I will be with him in trouble; I will deliver him, and honour him.
–Psalm 91:15

A new culture and getting to know a whole new set of people was difficult. We did not know many of the current missionaries. To aid our own adjustment period, we prayed a lot.

Prayers for Adjusting
- I missed my first grandbaby and daughters. I got so hot and tired. I prayed and cried.
- Language school was boring and difficult.
- Menopause compounded things.
- We had a bad bedbug infestation. That was so discouraging. We cleaned and cleaned and finally found chemicals to exterminate them.

Even though we were in the will of God, life was not easy.

Prayers for Salvation
It was rewarding to reach out to a new couple who came to church and see them seek the Lord. It was a challenge to mentor them and teach them the Word. It was a precious day when we knelt on the

dirt floor of their hut with prayers for God to forgive their sins and save their souls.

Jacklyn, a neighbor lady I loved, was dying of HIV. I visited her often. I hope to meet her in heaven someday. God heard her prayers.

Eleven-year-old Whinney, crippled from polio, had never been to school or church. A sweet lady from church became her tutor. Not only did Whinney learn to read, she also began memorizing verses. One day, she prayed for Jesus to come into her heart. There was rejoicing in heaven and in my heart.

Even though we were in the will of God, life was not easy.

There were also many disappointments. It was hard when people came to the Lord and then fell away. Some were dishonest and hypocritical.

Exodus chapters 2 and 3 tell us:

- God heard.
- God remembered.
- God looked upon them.
- God saw.
- God knew.
- God said, "Certainly I will be with you."

It helped me so much to hold onto the promises of God, to believe and to pray the promises.

Prayer is powerful! We all have a choice when confronted with cares. Will we fret and worry or will we pray and leave our cares in God's capable hands?

Will I choose prayer or panic?

Jesus, help me to not fall for the idea that because I am a child of God, life will be smooth. I believe You are with me through the storms and the sunshine.

Read Exodus 3:1-14

Boldness

Lord . . . grant unto thy servants, that with
all boldness they may speak thy WORD. –Acts 4:29

66 "I was discussing euthanasia with my co-workers," my son Markus mentioned to me. Shawna said, "I would be willing to kill myself so my children would not have to go through the same thing I went through with my mom."

Marcus said he told her, "Shawna, that's awful," and later she admitted to "just talking." "I actually would not hurt myself like that," she recanted.

Many of Markus's coworkers got into the conversation. The charge nurse had a different opinion: "I think everyone should have the right, if they are terminal, to kill themselves."

Markus said he was emphatic when he responded: "I dunno what you all believe about God, but He has a high moral standard! One of the Ten Commandments says: 'Thou shalt not kill' (Exod. 20:13). It doesn't say thou shalt not kill others. It also doesn't say thou shalt not kill yourself. It just says 'thou shalt not kill.' Life is sacred, and despite humans having the privilege of choice, it's still against God's law to take human life, be that your own or another's."

Are you bold and willing to speak for Jesus?

My friend Lorene, a nurse in the emergency room, said: "In conversations with my patients I try to find openings to share my faith. Last week, a lady remarked about my gray hair. I referred to what the Bible says about gray hair." I simply can't fathom how people live without God in their lives.

One of my sons shared that one day he awoke and was not enthused about going to work. He opened his Bible and read, "Give thanks." God helped his morning.

Think about your words and actions. Are you bold and willing to speak for Jesus? Can you encourage someone to embrace the gift of life? Can your words and actions uplift those discouraged with life? Pray for boldness.

May my words and actions, Lord, uplift those
who are discouraged with life.

Read Exodus 20:1-21

Forgive Him

*Therefore if thine enemy hunger, feed him; if he thirst,
give him drink: for in so doing thou shalt heap
coals of fire on his head.* –Romans 12:20

What do we need to do if we want God to forgive us? The Word of God teaches us to forgive. Forgiveness is not easy. We must have God's help to forgive and live in peace. When in Africa, I saw both forgiveness and unforgiveness. Women living in the African culture, and in any land, can choose to show revenge instead of forgiveness.

In Kenya:

- Women can choose a culturally acceptable norm—to leave in secret with crops from their fields, household items, and money and flee back to their homeland (house of their father) when there is marital strife.
- Throwing hot water may be a temptation.
- Most horribly, they may be tempted to put poison in their husband's food.

Women in any culture will choose to do good or ill in their marriage. In Romans 12:21 we find, "Be not overcome of evil, but overcome evil with good." Matthew 7:12 says, "Therefore all things whatsoever ye would that men should do to you, do ye even so to them: for this is the law and the prophets."

My father used to say, "The golden rule is for seven days of the week, twelve months of the year. It is found in Matthew 7:12." Do to others what you would like them to do for you.

What are we going to do with what we hear from the Word of God? Will we ask God to help us change to doing good for evil? When taught about being kind in marriage, one African lady remarked, "I am going to go home and wash my husband's clothes." This woman wanted to please God and be kind.

Nurture your relationship with love, respect, and kindness.

At Bible study one day, there was an old man sitting in the shade beside the mud hut. He sat apart from the others. Mary fixed a plate of food and carried it to the *Mzee* (term for an elderly man). He received it gratefully. Mary also threw a *mandazi* (a fried doughnut without a hole) to the dog. I saw the kindness of God in Mary that day.

Your husband is not your enemy, but your enemy will try to divide your union. Nurture your relationship with love, respect, and kindness.

Will you pray to love? Will you make deeds of love and kindness a daily habit?

God, help me to make giving love
and kindness a daily habit.

Read Romans 12

Encouraging Josephine

Say not thou, I will recompense evil; but wait on the LORD, and he shall save thee. –Proverbs 20:22

Josephine is a friend I met at the market in Ng'iya where I shopped for fruits, vegetables, and many other things. Josephine had a stall of seasonal produce: mangos, papaya, beans, and bananas. She walked for miles to get to the large open-air market.

I visited her home once. Her thatched-roof hut was located back in the country. Her husband, a big burly man, was glad to see us. He reminded me of an ox. It was an honor to them to have a white couple step inside their door. We shared Christian literature. She graciously served us white bread and a hot drink.

We always hoped that people who wanted to be friends were seeking God.

We always hoped that people who wanted to be friends were seeking God. Too often it seemed that the draw was to have a white friend.

One evening my phone rang. It was Josephine. She and her husband had a quarrel. "He got so mad he really beat me," she confided. (I do not understand how Kenyan men can beat their wives. For too many, it is a custom deeply engrained in their culture). She ran away from home, too afraid to stay. She had six children; the youngest were one-year-old twins.

What could I say? What should I do? I prayed for her over the phone. I did not know the way to her house or where she was hiding. The next day, I was surprised to meet Josephine at the market. She told me that a sister from her church had gone back home with her.

Later I asked the Kenyan ladies in my Sunday School class, "What would you say to encourage Josephine?"

- Prayer: ask God's help. There is power in prayer because our God is all-powerful.
- Treat him kindly. Do extra kind things. Cook well. Please him with hot chai in the morning.
- Speak softly (Prov. 15:1). Return good for evil. Follow Romans 12:17 and 21; conquer evil by doing good.
- God blesses those who are persecuted for doing right (see Matthew 5:10-12).
- We are not promised an easy life. God promises to be with us.

How is it that I am blessed? I have been given so much. My husband has never touched me in an unkind way. It would be unthinkable for him to beat me.

True followers of Jesus:

- Must be willing to give when others take.
- Love when others hate.
- Help when others abuse.
- Give up rights in order to serve others.
- Do good to all men.

Is there a Josephine in your life to encourage?

Relating to difficult people and circumstances
are times I always need You.

Read Matthew 5:38-48

A Big Heart

Take heed that ye despise not one of these little ones; for I say unto you, That in heaven their angels do always behold the face of my Father which is in heaven. –Matthew 18:10

A lady from Nakuru (Kenya) was talking about children with a friend. The African lady said, "Children are such a blessing, but many in Kenya no longer want to be bothered, especially with someone else's child."

This lady is married to a widower and knows what it is like to love another woman's children. They have five children and have also taken in orphaned and abandoned children. It is not always easy for them to have enough *pesa* (money) for food.

For example, a sixteen-year-old boy was kicked out of the house by his uncle's wife, who did not want to feed a child who was not her own. He wandered around the village; kindhearted folks gave him a bite to eat. He was sleeping in *choos* (outhouses). This caring couple opened their heart and home and gave the destitute lad food and shelter. They shared the little they had with someone who had less. "Pray that I can have a big heart," she shared. "Pray that God will make my heart big enough to love whoever God wants me to love."

Many people in Kenya care for orphans who are their relatives. Others treat orphans cruelly, and those unfortunate children become outcasts.

May God bless those in any land who have big hearts by caring for children in need. There are people who care about children and make a difference for Jesus by opening their doors to take in needy little ones.

Three little girls, triplets, walked into a graduation program with a family I knew. These small gals were in foster care, and the family was fostering to adopt. They were giving of their time and talents to make a difference for these dear girls.

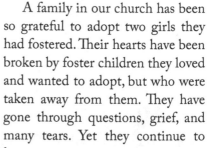

May God bless those in any land who have big hearts by caring for children in need.

A family in our church has been so grateful to adopt two girls they had fostered. Their hearts have been broken by foster children they loved and wanted to adopt, but who were taken away from them. They have gone through questions, grief, and many tears. Yet they continue to love and work with needy children.

What a beautiful way to have a big heart for Jesus.

In what ways do you have a big heart for Jesus?

Oh Father God, wherever I live,
may people see Your life in me.

Read Matthew 25:31-46

My Friends,
Kenyan Ladies

By this shall all men know that ye are my disciples, if ye have love one to another. –John 13:35

rayer requests at Bible study were most unique. Typical requests were for healing for a pain in my foot, a pain in my head, pain of the tooth, and on and on. I sigh as I hear these things. These dear African friends have many ailments and often no money to see a doctor. What would my prayer requests be if I were in their shoes? I appreciated when they requested prayers for people. Often prayer was requested for peace in their *dala* (homes).

It was a pleasant afternoon at Bible study held at Maurice's parents beautiful *dala* in the country. Later in the day, my son Micah and I boarded a modern airliner for the long flight to New York. I anticipated seeing a new grandson, daughters, and my future daughter-in-law. I looked forward to holding grandchildren and lending a helping hand.

I had informed the native ladies that I was leaving to help at my daughter's house in America. I thought of requesting prayer for our trip. I was so blessed when Maria requested prayer for our *safari* (journey). My heart was happy.

The ladies were warm and gracious as I hugged and kissed them goodbye. We talked about our flights. They were amazed that we would be served food and drink on the plane, and that there was even a *choo* (restroom). None of these precious country women would likely ever have the chance to fly the skies. They were interested in my travels and family, though they could not conceive of a thirty-hour trip spanning ten thousand miles.

Our hostess showed me a pretty red Iresine plant I had given her that was growing profusely beside her house. They shared their food with us. We cared about each other.

"In whatever mission model you work, people will know if you truly love them."

⌒

My friend Cynthia once remarked, "In whatever mission model you work, people will know if you truly love them."

My mind goes to lyrics from the song, "Therefore Give Us Love":

From the overshadowing, of thy gold and silver wing,
shed on us who to thee sing, holy heavenly love.

Love is kind and suffers long, love is meek and thinks no
    wrong,
love than death itself more strong, therefore give us love.[5]

Jesus, You love me so much, how can I fathom Your love?
Thank You, thank You, for loving me.

Read 1 Corinthians 13

---

[5] By Christopher Wordsworth (1807-1885). Public domain.

Never Lose Hope

*Happy is he that hath the God of Jacob for his help,
whose hope is in the LORD his God.* –Psalm 146:5

As I shared before, I like to have a word from God for each New Year. For 2015, I kept thinking about the word *hope*. Verses and sayings containing my word seem to jump out at me all year in encouraging ways.

Jesus died to save us, to strengthen us, to help us, and to give us hope. There is always hope when we honor God in our lives. There is nothing greater than God's power. He is able to heal us and provide for our needs.

We are not without hope. God is the source of all hope. God never leaves us to face our trials alone. Heaven is a future reality and hope for God's children. No matter how difficult life is now, there is hope for the future. Jesus will come back on the clouds for His children. His return gives us hope to persevere during tough times. Trust in Him. Possess the hope of meeting Him face-to-face. Jesus's name is hope for all the world.

I had hoped to enjoy life in Africa more, but I was determined to be faithful whether I did or not.

I choose to live into the purpose God has for me. First Corinthians 13:7 and 13 tell us that love "beareth all things, believeth all things, hopeth all things, endureth all things . . . And now abideth faith, hope, charity, these three; but the greatest of these is charity."

When we lived in Kenya, Mark and I felt it would be good if I would fly to New York and help our daughter after the birth of her second child. I hoped to go. Sometimes I shed tears and actually felt ill because I missed my daughters greatly. I longed to go visit, and I did not know if the mission board would grant permission. I lost weight. I tried to not set my heart on it or hope too much.

Jesus is the hope of all the world.

⟋⟍

The mission board eventually said yes. I called my daughter. In my relief and longing, I cried.

Proverbs 13:12 says, "Hope deferred maketh the heart sick: but when the desire cometh, it is a tree of life."

God is the God of hope and healing. Jesus is the hope of all the world.

Jesus, thank You for helping me choose to live in hope.

Read Psalm 147

Remember Jesus

That if thou shalt confess with thy mouth the Lord Jesus, and shalt believe in thine heart that God hath raised him from the dead, thou shalt be saved. –Romans 10:9

What will I do with Jesus? Will I embrace or reject Him as the ultimate authority? If I embrace Him, I am provided with the life-giving Word. If I reject Jesus, I open my heart to deception.

At His crucifixion:

- The crowd watched.
- Leaders scoffed.
- Soldiers mocked.
- Women cried as their Savior died.

The two thieves:

- One mocked.
- The other pled in faith, "Lord, remember me when thou comest into thy kingdom" (Luke 23:42).

Nothing is without notice to our Lord, who said, "Today shalt thou be with me in paradise" (Luke 23:43).

Jesus gave His life, the ultimate sacrifice and act of love. Even when dying, He remembered those who called on Him. He noticed the women's faithfulness, loyalty, and love at the cross.

Joseph requested His body, wrapped it, and laid it in the tomb.

The women watched. Early in the morning they brought spices to reverently anoint His body. Their Master and Lord was not in the tomb. Mary wept and Jesus said to her, "Woman, why weepest thou?" (John 20:15). Jesus saw her tears; He cared. Mary Magdalene was rewarded with being the first to greet the risen Lord.

The thief cried, "Lord remember me." God certainly remembers us.

I want to be more aware of the presence of Jesus each day. I can be intentional about verses on walls or mirrors to help guide my thoughts. I can choose to read His Word and know His words. I can share what Jesus has done for me with friends. I can point small children to the wonders of creation and say, "God made that beauty."

Jesus gave His life, the ultimate sacrifice and act of love.

My daughter shared, "A ribbon on my dish soap bottle is a reminder to turn my heart to God. I want to grow in practicing His presence. I want to talk to Him the first thing when I awaken. I want to turn my heart to Jesus when things get rough."

God remembers me. I want to remember Jesus. My goal, in life or death, is Jesus. Jesus is Emmanuel, God *with us*.

Do I remember Jesus?

Every day that I live, I want to remember You, Lord.

Read John 19:25-42

Cared For

*For God is not unrighteous to forget your work and
labour of love, which ye have showed toward his name,
in that ye have ministered to the saints, and do minister.*
—Hebrews 6:10

A "taller than their mother" son is on each side of me. Our
hands are full of pizza, salad, cookies, and fruit as we walk
down the compound lane for supper with Dean's family
before they leave for furlough. It is a pleasure to do things with my
sons.

Kindness does come back. When we moved to Ng'iya, I did not
know how I could manage all the work. On our last night in Kisumu, Dean's wife brought us a delicious hot meal.

I often thought of the example of Arthur and Lill, who reached
out to missionaries as well as to natives in El Salvador. They took
time to mentor youth who were away from their families. They truly
cared about all people.

One of the mission ladies was sick, again. I felt prompted to
take her ice-cold red Gatorade, a box of crackers, a pint of yogurt,
and a loaf of homemade bread. It was a bit difficult to give away the
bread, as baking in my small gas oven was an adjustment. "Lord," I
prayed, "take this food and flowers as a gift to you."

On a day when we were still new in Kenya, I was surrounded by
ordinary work in my house: cooking, baking, planning how to feed
hungry sons . . . I was sad and tears were lurking. Just then a friend
walked in with iced coffee. I shared frustrations and she shared
encouraging words, not pity. She was there for me, telling me where

to buy groceries, fresh spices, wheat flour, and she shared that bread could be purchased at a nearby bread shack. It was truly helpful to know where to purchase ordinary things.

Then one evening I stepped into her dark house while the youth played volleyball. She was ill and crying, and it was my turn to show support and care. I washed her dishes and prayed for her.

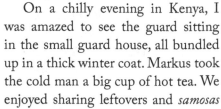

Wherever you live, care for someone for the love of Jesus.

On a chilly evening in Kenya, I was amazed to see the guard sitting in the small guard house, all bundled up in a thick winter coat. Markus took the cold man a big cup of hot tea. We enjoyed sharing leftovers and *samosas* (an African fried pastry filled with meat and vegetables) with the gatemen.

The youth came to our house one evening for singing practice. Our home was filled with the smell of fresh cinnamon rolls baking.

I count it a joy to share good food.

Wherever you live, care for someone for the love of Jesus.

Jesus, here, now, help me to know how to show love and care.

Read Hebrews 10

Only in Africa

Out of the depths have I cried unto thee, O Lᴏʀᴅ.
–Psalm 130:1

Early on a Saturday morning, Mark and I drove the few miles out to Hippo Point. Time with God and each other was good. The wonders of creation were an amazing bonus on this particular morning. I stood gazing across the peaceful waters of Lake Victoria, hoping to see a hippo.

"There is one," Mark breathed. We could see the hippo's huge head as he came up for air.

Morning time with God is so vital, both in Kenya and at home. Only God can help me cope with changes and stresses.

I enjoyed observing the birds too. We saw the Yellow Weaver bird, black and white Wagtails, small indigo Bluebirds, and a Kingfisher. The earth is full of the goodness of the Lord. Beauties of nature amid the poverty helped me cope.

These Diseases

My sons were away for two hours taking pictures of orphans. When they got home, the youngest had a fever and went straight to bed. He stayed there the rest of the day and awoke with an aching head. We had been in Kenya for five months, and he was ill again. The doctor feels certain it's malaria. She prescribed malaria meds. His fevers leave him sad and make him long to go back home.

I stayed home from church with him, and we listened to a CD by Rick Rhodes. I read good books aloud beside his bed. He was ill, off and on, for two weeks. One evening he had a headache yet again.

His older brother suggested we pray around his bed. I just whispered a prayer through my tears.

He slowly regained his health. A friend recommended vitamin C and probiotics.

Lord, I know You have all power to heal. I struggle with believing You will. Help my unbelief.

Mother Heart

We left Ohio with one son at home. Leaving him behind was hard on the heart of this mother. The changes were difficult. When I prayed for him during those first weeks in Africa, I often shed tears. *We are so far away. Lord, watch over him Lord, guard his heart and mind, draw him to yourself.*

> *Only God can help me cope with changes and stresses.*

An e-mail from him cheered me. He shared three important goals: Glorify God and grow in relationship with him. Build meaningful relationships with the deaf. Teach about God, teach Spanish.

"God has been helping me to keep a respectful attitude," he shared.

When I pray for our children, I ask God to accomplish whatever He has planned for each of their lives, wherever He leads.

I give my sons and daughters to You, Lord.

Read Psalm 5

What Kind of Visitor?

Whom I have sent unto you for the same purpose, that ye might know our affairs, and that he might comfort your hearts. –Ephesians 6:22

Ken and Christy came to visit church friends who were serving in Kenya. My daughter sent a dress and veils with them for me.

Christy brought the things over to our house. I showed her pictures of my daughters and suddenly tears flooded my eyes. She wondered if she could pray for me. With her arm around me, right then and there, she prayed. Her prayer and kind words were a blessing and gave me much encouragement.

Months later, Dave and Esther's family visited. It was delightful to have a family from Ohio. They treated us to supper at Kiboko Bay Resort. We had a great time eating at outdoor tables among the beautiful tropical foliage. One of their girls hoped to see a hippopotamus; the other daughter was scared. It was a jolly time. The next morning, we were happy to serve them breakfast in our carport. They cleaned the guest house before they left. It is a blessing when visitors clean up after themselves and take an interest in our lives.

Later, James and Rhonda and Lorene flew to Africa to visit. They helped with whatever duties needed to be done. We had worked with them in Belize in our youth. They cared about us, loved our sons, cooked meals, and reached out to natives. We met the native church ladies at two locations, at Juline's large house in the morning and later under a big mango tree at Maria's house for a time of sharing from the Word. Lorene, a nurse, spoke to the ladies about healthcare and gave them each a packet of health products. It was a special time we all enjoyed.

Our friends went with us to pass out Bibles and Bible storybooks at a hospital. Lorene even helped deliver a Kenyan baby. It was a lovely vacation to go to the Masai Mara with them as well. We thanked God for refreshing visitors.

We thanked God for refreshing visitors.

Do you have friends serving God in lands far away? If possible, visit them. For sure, pray for them and their children. Write a letter or an email to let them know of your prayers and interest in their lives.

If you have the opportunity to travel to a foreign land, what kind of visitor will you be?

Thank You so much, Father, for the gift of friends, friends who cared enough to put forth time and effort to travel ten thousand miles to come to Africa.

Read Ephesians 6

Church Cultures

*And let us consider one another to provoke unto love
and to good works.* –Hebrews 10:24

While I was sitting in the Kenyan church with its open sides and dirt floor, I watched as the people dropped their coins in a woven basket. Foreigners dropped many coins in the collection plate. Then a poor widow came by. She dropped in one small coin.

What would Jesus say about this? "I tell you the truth," Jesus said, "this poor widow has given more than the white people. They have given a tiny part of their surplus, but she, poor as she is, has given everything she has" (see Luke 21:3-4).

The widow in Kenya was living with little. If we possessed only what she owned, we would consider ourselves destitute. She had few resources to earn money. Her gift seemed small, but it was her all. She gave it willingly because she loved her Savior. She was happy with what she had. She was content with enough to eat. Jesus admired her gift. It was generous and sacrificial.

The total amount of the offerings at the Kenyan church was often under ten dollars. A typical Sunday found four to six dollars in the offering basket, unless there were visitors. Yet, if we compared their income with those in America, they may well have been giving as much or more.

Is Jesus calling each of us to increase our giving, whether it be money, time, or talents? What will I give to Him who gave His all for me?

The church group in Kenya had Bible Study on Wednesday afternoons at members' homes. Most of the people lived off the land and were self-employed. At night they seldom went away. They walked miles to attend Bible study or were glad when they could catch a ride from someone.

One afternoon, Bible study was held at Jacob and Monica's. Their *dala* (home) has many nice tall trees. The hut was warm in the afternoon heat and packed full of people waiting to hear the Word of God. To my astonished American mind, I saw Jacob sitting in a corner swaddled in a heavy brown winter coat. Some of the women were outside in the shade. I joined them under the shade tree to cope with the heat.

God has made all nations of one blood.

God has made all nations of one blood. He loves every nationality equally.

Would I have been willing to attend Bible study if I would have had to walk miles in the afternoon? Can we encourage each other in church attendance wherever we live?

*I want to remember, Lord, that You
love every person equally.*

Read Luke 21:1-4

My Beautiful Cousin

*And let the beauty of the LORD our God be upon us; and
establish thou the work of our hands upon us; yea, the work
of our hands establish thou it.* –Psalm 90:17

She showed me the small room where she loves to spend time
with the Lord each morning. There was her Bible, books,
a container of pens, a pretty basket with writing material,
and her prayer wall. I was intrigued. On this wall were maps and
mementos of people and places she remembers in prayer. There was
a printed paper about Kingdom Channels, a ministry that serves in
the Middle East, an article about South Sudan, photos, and information about missions and friends.

This cousin cares about people, about the work of God, and
about places she will never have the opportunity to visit. She goes
to these lands in prayer. She commented that people say they will
pray for someone when God brings them to mind. She said, "I don't
trust my mind that far and need a list to help me." She especially
prays for a niece who does not have a mother to pray for her. It is
important to her to keep learning new things, including how to
be a better Christian. She loves to read and shares her books with
family and friends.

My cousin is beautiful with a radiance that comes from Jesus.
We attended a wedding thirty minutes from their home and inquired if we could come for supper and the night. Even though

they knew five of their grandchildren would be there, they opened their doors, made room for us at their large table, graciously welcomed us, and served delicious food.

She follows the example of both her mother and my own, women who would not gossip and rarely said anything negative about other people. She is quick to tell people things she appreciates about them.

My cousin is beautiful with a radiance that comes from Jesus.

Her grandchildren are dear to her heart. All children are important. She stoops to their level, and they respond well to her soft voice as she delights in giving them time and attention. She reads good stories, plays games, blows bubbles, and talks to them. First graders can earn some money from her by reading books or memorizing scriptures. She was a school teacher and still encourages grandchildren and others to fill their minds with worthwhile reading material. Though her grandchildren do not live nearby, she keeps up connections with weekly e-mails, and they are so excited when Grandma sends them a big birthday box by mail.

Her granddaughter said, "I am learning from Grandma to be generous, to see the best in people, and to care about children."

My Jesus, Your example of loving
children is one I want to follow.

Read Proverbs 31

Make God Big

O God, thou art terrible out of thy holy places:
the God of Israel is he that giveth strength and power
unto His people. Blessed be God. –Psalm 68:35

I had a discussion with my five-year-old grandson who was worried that his grandpa could not find the road to the hardware store to meet his dad. I assured Adryan, "Your grandpa is smart. He can find the way; plus he has GPS."

Adryan confidently informed me, "My dad is smarter than grandpa!" His dad was his big hero.

A squirrel was climbing around in the maple tree in front of our house as Joel and I were watching. I asked him if he could climb like that in the tree. "No," my grandson informed me, "but my dad could."

Another small lad, Isaiah, once told me, "I already am what my father is. In play, I teach school."

It's a gift that small sons look up to their fathers, that they believe and trust them. They literally believe their father in everything.

Do I believe God implicitly and trust Him always?

Do we believe this about God our Father? "Our Father which art in heaven" is a prayer we often pray. Everything He says, everything He does, is always right. Is my Father BIG in my eyes? Do I believe God implicitly and trust Him always? *He is our Father.* As sons we are called to pray. God is our Father. We are chosen to be His family. God our Father has everything at His disposal.

How do you teach your children? How can you make God BIG? Deuteronomy 6:6-7 tells us to repeat God's commands again and again to our children. Parents are to talk about them when at home, on the road, going to bed, and when getting up. As you work, as you walk, talk about God. Verses 12-13 say, "Be careful to not forget the Lord, fear him and serve him" (paraphrased).

Make God a part of your everyday experiences. Teach your children diligently to see God in all aspects of life, not just those that are church-related.

Be diligent; be intentional in teaching your children. Don't neglect praying for them. God is the one who draws all men to him. Your children will eventually decide to either love or reject Jesus.

May God be BIG for yourself and for others.

Bless and strengthen all mothers, Lord,
that they would faithfully teach Your ways.

Read Matthew 6:9-34

Love Connections

If a man love me, he will keep my words: and my Father will love him, and we will come unto him, and make our abode with him. –John 14:23

A s Mark and I were waiting to board our Delta flight to Kansas, we noticed an Amish couple seated in the waiting area. We went over to chat. A connection existed between us because we ladies wore modest dresses, and both of us were covering our heads from respect to God and His Word.

Amazingly, on our flight, they were seated right behind us. She had one of my books and shared with me some of her story and how for twenty years she had been working on writing a book. She planned to publish her book at Carlisle Printing. I was impressed with her courage—the courage to share about her difficult childhood and the willingness to make herself vulnerable in the hopes of being able to help others. It was a pleasure to meet her.

The Atlanta airport is huge. Mark remarked that he saw a Mennonite woman in another area. Later on I saw her, too, and I went over to chat. Again, our veils and modesty were a good first connection. This lady was flying to Kansas with her husband to attend the same wedding we were. We each had six children, though her oldest child was the same age as our youngest.

Men still respect modest women.

I believe there is a blessing and protection found in following God's Word. My Kenyan friend Mary told me that when she started dressing modestly and wearing a veil, ungodly men did not trouble or flirt with her. Men still respect modest women. Mark and I were at Texas Roadhouse one evening. I was amazed at how often other men opened the door for me, even when I was with my husband.

Evelyn Miller wrote: "Consider with me; what does the veil symbolize? And what is Satan's agenda? Humility and submission are in serious conflict with rebellion and control. Might a desire to live before God in humility and submission provide a compelling incentive for a daughter of the King to be veiled?"[6]

Muslims are veiled to please Allah. They are staunchly determined to revere their leader. I wear my veil in reverence and obedience to the King of kings and Lord of lords, the Almighty God and Creator of the universe. My goal is to bring glory to Jesus by covering my hair. It is a privilege to be identified as a Christian woman.

I want to glorify and honor You, Lord, in all I say and do.

Read 1 Corinthians 11

---

[6] Evelyn Miller, *Feminine Beauty* (Biblical Mennonite Alliance, 2016), 82.

Warmed by Kindness

For I am not ashamed of the gospel of Christ: for it is the power of God unto salvation to every one that believeth; to the Jew first, and also to the Greek. –Romans 1:16

I settled into my seat on the Delta flight and remarked to the young Chinese lady beside me, "It's cold in here." She then graciously offered to share her blue flight blanket. I accepted. We sat there, warmed by kindness and a shared blanket.

I want to be a face of friendliness and kindness to those I meet when we travel. We chatted about family. She told us she had no brothers or sisters. Most Chinese families have only one or two children.

She gasped in surprise when I told her, "We have six children and seven grandchildren."

"Do they all come home for Christmas?" she questioned. She felt it would be overwhelming to have such a large group and so many people in the house. That was difficult for her to imagine.

The following day she would be back home in China. Her parents were so thrilled to have their only child come back. She told me she worked at an American company.

Are Bibles allowed in China? I was curious. She did well with English. Yet I was not sure she understood my question. Mark reached into his backpack and pulled out his large black Thompson Chain Reference Bible. I wonder if that was the first time she saw a Bible? I opened the pages to John 3:16 and told her this is its most-loved verse. She pulled out her phone and took a picture. Then I turned to the first pages, and she snapped a picture of the title. We encouraged her to buy a Bible. I hope she found one in the Atlanta airport.

I want to be a face of friendliness and kindness to those I meet when we travel.

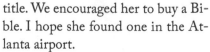

ble. I hope she found one in the Atlanta airport.

We drank coffee and tea; she watched a movie and slept. I wished I had remembered to put tracts in my purse. When it was time to de-board our flight, I told her, "In America we say, 'God bless you.'" She replied, "God bless you too." She walked out of the jetliner, out of my life, and disappeared into the sea of humanity.

Do my words draw people to Jesus?

So many people I only see once, Jesus; help me seize opportunities to speak for You.

Read 1 Corinthians 5

The Sad Old Man

*If thy brother be waxen poor, and fallen in decay with thee;
then thou shalt relieve him: yea, though he be a stranger, or a
sojourner; that he may live with thee.* –Leviticus 25:35

Mark and I were in town on a Friday evening. I was shopping at ALDI. It's always nice to find good prices on groceries. After I paid for my purchases and returned the cart, I saw an old man in front of the store. He was leaning against a large trash can with his jug of milk sitting on top of it. I kindly inquired, "Are you waiting on someone?"

"No," he said, "I just don't want to go home."

I didn't know what to say. "Jesus loves you," I told him. That sounded so trite. In retrospect, I wish I had taken time to talk more. I could have told him that we have a Father in heaven who cares about us, and whatever problem or situation we face, we can cry to God. I don't think I did well with that lonely man. I can pray for him. So quickly, though, I forget. Will God send another sad old man my way?

The Odd Ones
As we drove into the parking lot at Walnut Creek Cheese to eat lunch with our youngest son, I glanced toward the road and saw something odd. A man was pulling a loaded small red wagon and headed down State Route 39 on this hot day. An employee I knew

was pushing carts together outside the store. I paused to chat for a moment, to say I was happy to see him at work again. Then he said, "Did you see that man going down the road with the wagon? He told me he's walking from Cleveland to Washington, D.C.," he informed me. "I asked him if he needed any water. He told me he had water, but would like some cheese. So I went inside and bought cheese for him."

Jesus, we need Your compassion. Give us hearts of care.

Many Christians saw that man walking down the road pulling his wagon. A relative of mine noticed him resting under a shade tree at ProVia. A man from church saw him in the evening, miles farther down the route at the Schilling Hill Road intersection.

Did anyone invite him in for food or offer a bed? It seems we too easily fear the odd people. All people are loved by our Father. It's so easy to pull our rich, righteous robes around us and turn the other way.

> *Jesus, we need Your compassion.*
> *Give us hearts of care.*
> *Faces of love,*
> *Hands of kindness,*
> *Help us to show our love to You,*
> *By loving others.*

Read Hebrews 13

What Do
You Want?

*God is faithful, by whom ye were called unto the fellowship
of his Son Jesus Christ our Lord.* –1 Corinthians 1:9

Jesus knew what the blind man wanted and needed. Yet He wanted the poor man to ask, to express his needs to Him. What can I learn from this blind man?

- He cried out to Jesus in faith.
- He knew Jesus was the Messiah.
- He knew what he wanted.
- He did not listen to the crowd.

Jesus heard his longing cries and stopped to ask, "What do you want me to do for you?"

The blind man responded, "Lord, I want to see."

Satan tries his best to hinder people who are seeking. He used the crowd to discourage the blind man who needed Jesus's mercy. In the same way, he can use those close to us to discourage us.

What do I want Jesus to do for me? He longs for me to express my needs to Him.

It helps to write out specific prayers and praises on a notecard. Last week I needed to apologize to Mark numerous times. I wrote on my note card, "Jesus help me be a sweeter wife: not giving so much advice, allowing him to lead."

No matter how desperate my situation may be, when I call out to Jesus in faith, He will help me. Isaiah 53:5 says that He was beaten so I could be whole. He was whipped so I could be healed.

My Jesus knows just what I need. He wants me to tell Him those needs.

Share with a Friend

One woman remarked, "We are all wounded people." This is something I know well. A friend has a sister who is mentally ill. There is mental illness and a broken marriage among my siblings too. There may be the same in yours. Another friend was abandoned as a small child.

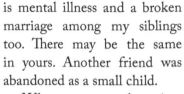

No matter how desperate my situation may be, when I call out to Jesus in faith, He will help me.

When one person hurts in a family, everyone aches. I wonder what each of you have that is difficult to bear? Sometimes we do not know because we do not know each other. We do not trust each other enough to share.

We need God. We need each other. We were not meant to walk alone in the journey of life.

Can we love each other enough that we are willing to listen, hear, and bind up the wounds of our friends for Jesus? There is strength in caring and praying together through our wounds and weaknesses.

God, thank You that You never leave us alone. Help us to walk with others. Give us friends to encourage us.

Read Luke 18:39-43

No Greater Joy

*I have no greater joy than to hear that my
children walk in truth.* –3 John 4

The neighbor's children start school this morning: they are beaming with fresh new clothes and anticipation. Their backpacks are filled with sharp pencils and colorful crayons.

One morning years ago, our five children were all ready for a new school year. They lined up, clean and shining, for a photo in front of our house. My parents were here.

"I have no greater joy than that my children walk in the truth." I can still hear my dad say those words. He loved his grandchildren, and they loved him.

A yellow bus screeched to a stop and opened its mouth; they filed in by age and were off. The school doors soon engulfed them. Another year was on its way. A special lunch was ready for them when they came home. It was important to me to be here to welcome them back.

Today we have grandchildren. School days have disappeared through a haze of fog called years. The years seem to have gone by so fast. As if by a magic touch, the children changed from small to adult to going out of our doors. Our oldest grandson is excited about being a scholar now.

> *"I have no greater joy than that my children walk in the truth." I can still hear my dad say those words.*

Tears cloud my vision this morning. I know God has been good to me. Yet we all have situations, wounds, and battle scars that rend our hearts. Will I continue to offer up my life as a continual living sacrifice to Him who loves me? God isn't finished with me yet. There is still work to be done in His kingdom. I do not want to live selfishly. I want a heart to continue serving Jesus, to care about and take time for people.

In the same way the children were excited about school, I want to embrace this season of life and throw my heart and soul into living each day for Jesus.

If you have school children, do your best to make home a happy place. Instill godly values. Teach scripture. May they see in you a passionate love for Jesus and an unquenchable love for them.

Jesus, help me to live well today.

Read 2 Timothy 3

Meaningful Ways

I thank my God upon every remembrance of you.
–Philippians 1:3

Married women can get bogged down with the work of raising a family. Single women grow weary of working to support themselves and can be lonely in their calling. When married and single women meet in meaningful ways, both are encouraged and cared for.

Vicky, a traveling nurse, worked at a hospital in Kansas so she could spend time with her grandmother and other relatives. She reached out to a mother with two small children and offered to babysit. The mother was truly grateful that she could go shopping alone while her husband was at an auction. The nurse's life was brightened by the interaction with lively little ones.

She served a supper of special foods typically served in Israel for an aunt and uncle and cousins. All who sat at that table were pleased to be there.

The thought of never having children can be a bitter pill for single women. I so much appreciate how one of my friends, a nurse, reaches out to our children. She cares about our grown sons and prays for them. One of our sons started a career in nursing. My friend has con-

Instead of waiting for someone to reach out to you, ask God for ideas of ways to connect meaningfully with others in ways that bless them.

nected with him and spoken truth, encouragement, and caution in his life. My heart is grateful.

Two single ladies in church share my birthday month. It is a tradition to meet for lunch to celebrate. It is so valuable to take time to connect with friends in church and to take an interest in each other's lives.

Each of us longs to be loved, wanted, and needed in relationships. Instead of waiting for someone to reach out to you, ask God for ideas of ways to connect meaningfully with others in ways that bless them. I am grateful for friends who invite me over for tea or coffee. I am grateful for those who initiate meeting and sharing heart to heart.

Authors Ann Spangler and Lois Tverberg, in *Sitting at the Feet of Rabbi Jesus*, share: "Look for opportunities to connect with others in meaningful ways, especially since modern culture seems to be spiraling in on itself with each person becoming more isolated."[7]

We need each other. We need to hear the stories of how God is working in our friends' lives. We can magnify the Lord by sharing answers to prayers and blessings. Take time to meet in meaningful ways.

I want to magnify You, Lord, by sharing answers to prayer.

Read Romans 16

---

[7] Ann Spangler and Lois Tverberg, *Sitting at the Feet of Rabbi Jesus* (Grand Rapids: Zondervan, 2018), 93.

Refreshed

If any man minister, let him do it as of the ability
which God giveth: that God in all things may be glorified
through Jesus Christ, to whom be praise and dominion
for ever and ever. Amen. −1 Peter 4:11

E arly one morning I drove two hours with Mark to Middle-
field, Ohio, to service the Lantern Book racks in that area.
First we met Freeman and Mary at a nice hometown
restaurant for breakfast. We learned to enjoy and appreciate friendship with them when we worked together in Kenya. It was refreshing to spend time together. It's such a blessing when friendships are
reciprocal. We care deeply about their family and work in Kenya.
They in turn inquire about our lives.

Over coffee, eggs, toast, and bacon, we poured out our hearts
to each other. We ended with holding hands for prayer, committing our lives anew to Jesus, and praying
for their flights back to Kenya the next *It's such a blessing*
morning and their work in Africa.

We were going to treat our friends. *when friendships*
Our waitress came and wanted the bill
returned that she had given to Mark. *are reciprocal.*
She informed us that a man at the
restaurant had anonymously picked up
the tab. I wondered if that man goes to the restaurant with eyes and
ears open, asking God to show him who to bless? What a sweet
surprise. Why did they choose to gift our meal? We were amazed
and grateful.

One Christmas when we were home on furlough, Freeman's family spent time at our house in Ng'iya. Even though they were on vacation, Freeman reached out to native Christians in our area. We were encouraged each time they visited us. We enjoyed numerous meals at their house as well. It is such a blessing when missionaries care and appreciate each other.

Mary shared this thought in an e-mail: "Wherever you are, there are relationships to deal with, but God's work can go on if we have Him first in our lives."

Refresh your friends.

How can I be a refreshing friend? I need Your help, Lord.

Read Romans 15

Enjoyed, Shocked

*Holy, holy, holy, is the LORD of hosts;
the whole earth is full of his glory.* –Isaiah 6:3

If you have an opportunity to live in a foreign culture, count yourself privileged. There are so many new things to see and observe. And if your heart is a heart of love, there will be many new friends.

In Kenya, I Enjoyed:

- Singing with sewing class ladies. Singing with children. Singing was a connection I cherished. Traditional African songs are unique. I liked hearing the children sing their African songs and enthusiastically sing American songs.
- I learned to love the African women. It was mutual. We appreciated and encouraged each other.

> *If your heart is a heart of love, there will be many new friends.*

- Working with my grown sons in the kitchen.
- Memorization projects with children.
- Sharing my plants and flowers.
- Making a difference in the life of crippled Whinney.
- Teaching Sunday School.
- The wonders of creation in Africa, the gorgeous tropical plants and flowers. Seeing a full moon rising behind the swaying banana trees was awesome.

- Shopping the outdoor African markets for fruits and vegetables was a cultural experience. I loved their handcrafted items and my friends there.
- Opportunities to encourage American and African women.

In Kenya, I Was Shocked:

- That many girls and women have clean-shaven heads.
- That polygamy is alive and well.
- At the amount of begging. What was I to do?
- At the untruths. The blatant lies were so discouraging.
- That too much reverence was given to whites.
- Concept of time, which was so different from ours.
- When I first saw a squat pot, no seat in the outhouse, just a hole in the ground.
- At snotty noses wiped on children's clothes.

Wherever we live, there will be blessings and hard things. Writing daily in a gratitude journal can help us focus on the good.

Thank You Jesus, I have so many blessings;
there is beauty everywhere I go.

Read Psalm 8

Summer Fruits

Behold, I have given you every herb bearing seed, which is upon the face of all the earth, and every tree, in the which is the fruit of a tree yielding seed; to you it shall be for meat.
—Genesis 1:29

I know how rich I am. I know that my truest wealth is Jesus. Knowing Jesus, loving Jesus, being loved, cared for, provided for, and looking forward to eternity with Jesus is the truest wealth.

It's July. I am rich in so many other ways too. Take, for instance, fresh fruits. I just bought more fruit for an outdoor hymn singing for our Sunday evening. I was asked to bring fruit. I enjoy fruit and foods that promote health.

Currently we have sweet Michigan blueberries, cherries, bananas, oranges, kiwi, lemons, juicy and delightful peaches, and organic apples! We picked the last of the fresh black raspberries from our patch. That's nine fresh fruits. We have so much good food. Every day we have enough for three meals, and snacks if we wish. My house is full of food.

Jesus, help me to forever be grateful, most of all for You.

I have not only fruits; I also have fresh lettuce, cabbage, potatoes, peppers, broccoli, onions, peas, red beets, green beans, and surely I am missing some more.

Oh yes! I thought of fresh garlic, sweet corn, and tomatoes still growing. Zucchini is shooting out on the vines. Radishes and

mushrooms are popping up. All of the previously-mentioned produce is in my house or garden. That's many more than nine fresh
vegetables. It's an amazing bounty, either from my garden or purchased at nearby markets.

How is it that we have much? In many other countries there is
little. People are hungry; some are starving for food to eat. Multi-
tudes are starving for Jesus. Who cares enough to go and share with
them? Who cares enough to share Jesus wherever they live?

Jesus, help me to forever be grateful, most of all for You. You
love me; You died for me.

I determine to be grateful for ordinary and for many extraor-
dinary gifts. You have given me fruits and the abundance of foods
from the earth, created by You, to be received with thanksgiving.

You have given me the gift of family, church, and so many caring
friends.

*Thank You, Jesus for Your love, the richness of salvation, and
all the array of amazing foods You have provided.*

Read Psalm 33

My Lovely Friend

*But now thus saith the LORD that created thee, O Jacob, and
he that formed thee, O Israel, Fear not; for I have redeemed
thee, I have called thee by thy name; thou art mine.*
–Isaiah 43:1

"Cultivating an awareness of God is important for me to
nourish my relationship with Him," said my lovely
single friend. She continued:

It's not just during my quiet time, but throughout my
day. When I see beauty, I see God. When my thoughts go
to people and situations, I try to pray. When I'm confronted with challenges, I cry out to God for wisdom and grace.
The awareness of God and
my quiet time are most important to me. Disciplines
are a part of my life. Memorizing scripture takes
more work now than it
used to. I still value memorization. Exercise. Eating
healthy food. Getting ad-
equate sleep. Those things
impact how I feel physical-
ly and help me to nourish my relationship with God. . . .

*Can I, as a married
woman, learn to reach
out, care and speak
to my single friends in
meaningful ways?*

[I also know that] loving others is key in relationships. I
struggle with that. It's hard in our culture to feel that I am

someone of value as a single lady. Without a proper self-image, it's hard to put myself out there and be friendly. Today someone was telling me about a friend who just started dating. I was told the friend was deserving of a boyfriend. It wasn't verbalized that I'm undeserving because I am single, but it left me feeling undeserving. It's hard for me not to let things like that affect my self-image. I wonder, do I hurt people and not realize it? I'm confident that lady didn't mean to be unkind to me. A friend at church remarked, "You single ladies are such a blessing to the church." But a visitor lady remarked that I am "just a leftover blessing." I pray that God would guide my tongue and heart so I can be sensitive to others. I'd rather be on the receiving end of something hurtful then being the one giving it.

I appreciated my friend's comments. Can I, as a married woman, learn to reach out, care and speak to my single friends in meaningful ways? I need and appreciate them. They need married friends too.

Both married and single women need Jesus. Jesus gives us joy. Jesus is the One who makes us lovely whether we are married or single.

I love my friends who have never married;
bless and encourage them today, Jesus.

Read Isaiah 62

Time to Nurture

Bring them up in the nurture and admonition of the Lord.
–Ephesians 6:4

What do we take time to nurture?

Nurture means the care and attention given to help growth and development. It is to nourish, to provide food and other things needed to live and be healthy. Do we care enough to take time to nurture what is important?

Nurture Health
Health is enhanced if we make good choices:

- Choose healthy foods and less sugar.
- Choose to drink lots of water.
- Be willing to work and exercise.

Nurture a Relationship with God
Walking with God requires choices:

- I will love God's Word and read it every day.
- I will be aware of God and His blessings.
- I will praise Him in the beauties of nature.

Nurture Children
Parenting is not easy. It is a constant task, a daily action. God's Word says, "Children, obey your parents" (Eph. 6:1). Are they going

to teach themselves obedience? Whose responsibility is it to teach obedience?

I remember twenty-five years ago I was discouraged with naughty small boys when Mark was leaving for school. He encouraged me to not give up. We cannot give up.

Take time to nurture what is important.

❧

Small children can learn God's Word. Post verses on your kitchen and bedroom walls. Review them at mealtimes and at night when you tuck them into bed. When you go away, recite verses together. Nurture your children by teaching obedience and God's Word. Give plenty of hugs, kisses, and stories.

Nurture Husbands
Marriage is for life, designed by God.

- Choose to love and be kind to one another and make being together good.
- Choose to be intentional for the health of your marriage.

Will you cherish, show affection and keep and cultivate love? Mark's parents were married nearly sixty years. One evening they were holding hands as they walked down the sidewalk to our house. I love that example.

Nurture your relationship with your husband. Don't pour all your love and energy on your children to his neglect. Life is ever full of change. Someday it will be just you and your husband at home. Stay both by your husband's side and on his side. If you stick up for your children against him, it may fatally wound your home and marriage.

I want to nurture health, Lord, but most of all my relationship with You and others.

Read Titus 2

A Mother-in-Law Manual

She openeth her mouth with wisdom; and in her tongue is the law of kindness. –Proverbs 31:26

Is there a "How to Be a Good Mother-in-Law" manual? Does the Bible speak into this area of my life? My thoughts went to Ephesians 4:32: "Be ye kind one to another."

In my heart, I long to relate well as a mother-in-law. I want to be kind. How can I show kindness and care? One day I had the idea to ask if I could come over for a few hours to help my daughter-in-law with anything she wanted done. I was happy she wanted me to come. When I got there, my small grandson was sitting on his highchair with his breakfast. I sat at the table and asked advice about what to do about my earache? She gave good suggestions, including a drop of lavender on cotton to stuff in my ear. It was quite dear that my charming grandson copied me, and soon his ear sported a tuft of white cotton.

No woman is perfect. I know I am not. I want to be accepted for who and what I am. Can I extend that to those who marry into our family? There are many things I appreciate about my daughter-in-law. She is a good mother. She loves to garden. We all like green growing things. It's nice to work together in the greenhouse. She is efficient in many, many areas. She loves my son! (I wrote this when I had one daughter-in-law.)

Babysitting is a good connection too. I enjoy seeing Mark enjoy being a grandfather. The sunshine of a small child is good for our home. I read to our grandson; we sing and watch the birds.

When I have concerns, I want to be a mother-in-law who prays. I want to focus on what is good and not try to control my married children's lives; I could not anyway. Scripture teaches that a man should leave his father and mother.

May our lives be marked by kindness.

One sweet thing my daughter-in-law did was treat me for a late Mother's Day meal. We liked the setting and food of Amish Country Doughnuts. I appreciate when my daughter-in-law takes time to do things with me, and I want to do things with her.

The Bible tells us that a man should leave his father and mother and cleave to his wife. We need to allow our children to leave. They are responsible to God, no longer to us as parents.

What kind of mother-in-law am I?

If you are a young woman, what kind of daughter-in-law are you?

May our lives be marked by kindness.

Lord, may my life be marked with kindness
and acceptance for daughters-in-law.

Read 1 Timothy 1

Life Overseas

Casting all your care upon him; for he careth for you.
−1 Peter 5:7

A friend shared an experience while living in West Africa:

My husband went out on Friday evening while I was in the house putting the boys to bed. As he was coming home, he thought it sounded like I was running a vacuum cleaner inside. As he approached our door to come inside he realized the noise was now behind him. He turned to see an angry snake writhing around on the concrete. It was a carpet viper. When upset, they rub their scales together. He slashed it to death with our cutlass. We think our cat was playing with it before he came home; maybe that is why it was making all that noise. We have seen this type of snake before. They are common in West Africa, and very poisonous. We thank God for His protection!

Another friend's missionary experience:

One of my washers has not been working for over a month. It has been rainy, so the wash pile has never disappeared because we never can get enough loads done in a day. It has been hard. A family of ten has so much laundry. Finally, the technician called today and said he had the new control board the washing machine needed. As he and my husband were pulling the machine apart to change the board, they realized the real problem was chewed wires. Rats had been in the washing machine and had the time of their lives. I'm hopeful that gorging themselves led to a swift death by electrocution, but probably not.

Lesson learned? Who knows, except to keep rat bait under the washing machine.

My washing machine may have been the only one in the area when we lived in the interior of Kenya. The yardman and his wife were fascinated. Many Kenyans wash their clothes efficiently by hand. Months later, the washing machine malfunctioned. For American women, it is not easy to scrub clothes by hand. The yardman's wife lent a hand and happily washed anything for me.

Prayer, trust, and a grateful heart please our Father everywhere we go.

An energetic work team from Belle Center, Ohio, visited us in Kenya. The men helped pour concrete for a back porch. Work flew by as the girls cleaned the house, washed windows, and made pear sauce. They offered to take a big load of laundry to the guest house and wash it for me. I appreciated their kindness.

We never saw a big snake in our yard. Our fenced-in yard with a dog helped. I prayed for God's hand of protection often. I watched as the yardman killed a green poisonous snake not far from our house.

There are dangers in every land. There are ordinary frustrations here and there. Prayer, trust, and a grateful heart please our Father everywhere we go.

Everywhere I go, You, Lord, are always with me.
I rejoice in that promise.

Read James 1

Edifying Books

Let the words of my mouth, and the meditation of my heart,
be acceptable in thy sight, O LORD, my strength,
and my redeemer. –Psalm 19:14

I love to read. I love God's Word. His Word is life. It strengthens me and prepares me for my days. His Word gives me hope and direction.

My diet consists of a big variety of books: inspirational, nonfiction, historical, missionary stories, and more. I choose to not read much fiction. I value books that challenge and encourage me. How can I ever be bored when I love to read? Is there such a thing as too much reading time? My days are filled up with many duties, not just books.

Carefulness in what I read and meditate on is important to me.

At a yard sale in the spring there were, as usual, many books. I quickly scanned the titles and purchased one. I thought it sounded like an interesting true story. It was a fanciful tale of a man who lied about having a girlfriend so he could please the man who wanted to hire him for a teaching position. I found the book intriguing. I never finished it though, because it became too graphic. Too

Mothers have a big responsibility to help children choose edifying books.

many books are too frank and free about sex. The book ended up in the trash can.

Recently I heard a minister lament about a young couple from

Christian homes who married, but after some years separated. It was questioned if the girl had no warning about the type of man he was. Sadly, he had been involved in pornography. Pornography opens a person's heart and mind to the powers of darkness and demons.

The young lady was also not guiltless. She had been taken up with romance novels. Novels create unrealistic expectations in the minds of youth and married women. What a sad combination that contributed to a broken home.

Years ago, I was shocked to see the kind of books a young Christian woman was checking out at the library. Mothers have a big responsibility to help children choose edifying books.

Oh, that we would spend time filling their minds with the Word of God and literature that would inspire and lead to more godliness.

What about you and I? Is what we read an example to our friends?

Jesus, My Redeemer, I want to fill my mind
with the goodness of Your Word.

Read Philippians 4:1-8

Be an Encourager

*The lips of the righteous feed many: but fools die
for want of wisdom.* –Proverbs 10:21

God encourages us through friends. He encourages us through our children. He encourages us through His Word. Am I taking time to encourage anyone? This note from a friend put golden sunshine in my day:

> We enjoyed the soap making day at your house! What a blessing and encouragement it is to interact/fellowship with ladies older than myself that love the Lord. If you ever wonder, your life does make a difference. I appreciate your friendship and example.

Twenty-four years ago, my seven-year-old daughter placed a yellow sticky note on my pillow. I am grateful I saved it. Here are her endearing words: "I love you MOM, I will pray for you that Marcellus will sleep all night. Thank you for stuff you do for me. Lynita, age 7."

In my Bible is a faded yellow sticky note that says, "I love you mom (age 35.) I love you very much" (Margretta, age 5).

My children are grown. How the times change. My daughter has four children, and the oldest is five. I pray for her that her children could sleep well and that she could too.

One day, my son Markus drove past our neighbor Antonia's on his way home from work. He saw that her goat (Leona) was out, so he called her. "Turn around and come back," she said, "I have something for your mom." Markus went back; he told Antonia he needed hot tea. She joyfully made tea and sent a loaf of fresh bread for me. She encouraged both of us.

How has God encouraged you? He encourages me often through friends and family. God's Word encourages and gives me hope. He encourages me in many ways. I

How has God encouraged you?

also feel His goodness in the beauty of nature and awe-inspiring ribbons of gold and red in gorgeous sunsets.

So easily we get distracted from what is most important. Do we really believe we should take time for people? What would happen in our lives if the first thing we reached for was God's Word, and the last thing we held before we went to bed was His Word? Would we become so filled with God that His goodness and kindness would overflow to everyone we met?

How long does it take to write a note? If God reminds you, take time. Be an encourager.

Help me to do what You prompt me to do, Lord.

Read Proverbs 10

Influence Others

Even so must their wives be grave, not slanderers, sober, faithful in all things. –1 Timothy 3:11

Women have a big influence on their husbands. Do I appreciate him and let him know? Or am I pulling him down?

God wants His children to love and encourage each other in our homes, churches, and in our walks with Jesus. If you are an older lady, are you willing to be a friend to a younger woman and speak into her life? If you hear a hint of difficulties in her marriage, especially if you are already friends, you have an opportunity to share words and encourage her to love her husband and do him good. She will know if you genuinely care. Pray for her and pray with her. Share books that have helped you in your marriage.

We need care within the church. We need care for those who do not know the Lord outside of church.

After my daughters were married, one day I was bemoaning that I had no one to help me make applesauce. A young married lady heard and offered to come help. Thankfully, I allowed her to do that. Now I like the tradition of going to her house each fall and helping her can pears. Working together initially forged our friendship, and that continues even today. Working alongside one another helps us know and understand each other.

We cannot expect perfection in a church. Hopefully, we are in a church with brothers and sisters who love God, seek God, and care about each other. We need care within the church. We need care for those who do not know the Lord outside of church. Who will you influence?

I want to take time for people, Jesus, and not
just be consumed with my own life.

Read Colossians 3

Seize Opportunities

And that from a child thou hast known the holy scriptures,
which are able to make thee wise unto salvation through
faith which is in Christ Jesus. –2 Timothy 3:15

A friend shared how the mother of two small boys for whom she babysat always had something kind and encouraging to say. She would ask me what God has been doing in my life and always encouraged me to keep walking with the Lord and to desire obedience to His calling. When I quit teaching school and did not know what to do next, my friend told me I was at a beautiful place in life, waiting on the Lord to direct my next step.

This lady reaches out to ungodly neighbors by inviting them over for a meal. She asks God to give her an opportunity to inquire about their lives. She cares about people. She is also supportive of her husband, who does some things that she does not completely understand. She told me once that she wants to submit and come under his authority.

Mothers have golden opportunities to impress God's truth in their children's hearts.

I love the way she speaks truth into the lives of her small sons, who are three and seven. Her brother was going through a divorce. She explained to her sons why divorce is wrong, and she read scripture to them about divorce being a sin. I thought they were too young to understand such scriptures. She always said it is important to teach them when she has the opportunity rather than wait until it is too late.

Mothers have golden opportunities to impress God's truth in their children's hearts. Children are influenced by watching their parents live out the Word of God. Children are intuitive and know when parents are for real.

At a family seminar in Kenya, our friend Jason shared:

> It is a parent's responsibility to make home a safe place. The wife and children need protection. It is the father's job to be a watchman and provide physical, emotional, and spiritual protection. Show God to your children. Intercede for them in prayer. Their father, too, needs to be submitting to the authority of God, and the wife to the authority of her husband.

Teach while the clay is soft and pliable in your hands. Teach and ask the Lord for wisdom.

Lord, give fathers and mothers wisdom to
influence their children for Jesus.

Read 1 Timothy 1

Remote Places

*Ye shall be witness unto me both in Jerusalem,
and in all Judea, and in Samaria, and unto
the uttermost part of the earth.* –Acts 1:8

A friend of mine has many opportunities to visit remote places when they travel with medical teams. She shared that women in a remote area of Kenya had a couple of recurring questions:

- Can you breastfeed while pregnant?
- Will it harm the baby in the womb?
- Is there a way to practice natural family planning that does not involve abstinence?

A woman's health and desires are hardly considered in that culture. My friends shared:

The question session with the old midwife in attendance was fascinating. They told me if they bleed too much after birth that they slaughter a ram and drink the blood to appease the bleeding. They also tie a string tight around the wrists.

When I told them about massaging the uterus until it became firm to control bleeding, they looked amazed. Even the man interpreting stopped and looked at me and gave an exclamation. He was a schoolteacher and learned something he had never known before.

But the most heartrending question of all was when the women told me they wanted to know about salvation. I asked them what they wanted to know about salvation. The day was Sunday, and I wasn't sure which of the women went to church. The women replied, "We need someone to tell us. We don't know what happens to us after we die."

My friend had a golden opportunity to speak into the lives of those women who live in remote places. Their family also shared Bible storybooks supplied by Christian Aid Ministries.

Foreign Foods

Experiences of those working foreign missions are enlightening, and they help us appreciate our own lives. They help us understand other cultures better. One young lady on a short-term mission trip shared:

Seize the opportunities God gives you.

I had the opportunity to go to their fields various times with friends in Ghana. This was very interesting and fun. I enjoyed helping carry yams on my head, observing the happy banter among my friends, and the raw experience of actually tasting a rat they killed and cooked in our process of doing field work. I also watched the killing of a cobra snake and found it amusing to see the ladies recoil in horror. It made me feel good to see they are scared of snakes too. When I see the intense manual labor they do to simply live sometimes these people seem invincible. I know this isn't true, but to my eyes, it can appear that way.

Seize the opportunities God gives you.

God, help me to embrace new experiences, new people, and even new foods for You.

Read 1 John 3

Her Canon
of Praise

I will praise thee, O Lord my God, with all my heart: and I will glorify thy name for evermore. –Psalm 86:12

I was blessed with the grateful spirit of this mother, a missionary friend from Africa, who shared a list of things she is thankful for. A grateful spirit brightens any home, whether on foreign or familiar soil.

As we reflect on the past year, here are a few things we are thankful for:

- What'sApp, cool rainy mornings, Jesus's perfect example of servanthood, safety during our many travels on poor roads and rivers.
- For the bore hole well that provides us with gallons of clean water.
- Our roof stayed on all through the storm season.
- The girls who help haul our water and wash our clothes.
- For watermelon being sold in our village during the worst of my morning sickness.
- The harmony of the four gospels.

A grateful spirit brightens any home, whether on foreign or familiar soil.

- Our worshipful songs playlist; the lush green all around during the rainy season.
- Days that we have good internet; for the starscapes and sunsets we enjoy here.
- Iced coffee on hot mornings. A plentiful yam harvest from our garden. The two owls that regularly sit in our trees in the evening.
- Our headlamp, the book of Nehemiah, fresh boiled peanuts.
- Our dear son who turned three this past month!
- Supporters who sacrificially love, pray, and give.
- Our Medscape (medical app).
- Electricity and fans.
- Joshua 1:8: Our motto that has taken us many miles in the past three years.
- Books—especially *Long Days of Small Things* by Catherine McNeil and *Planting Churches in Muslim Cities* by Greg Livingstone.
- Mosquito nets (they give one a real sense of security in this not-so-tight house).
- The discomforts of a kicking fetus.
- People responding to the Good News.
- Family who encourage us wholeheartedly.
- Red wildflowers growing in our yard.
- Our generous and hospitable village.
- The privilege of serving Jesus.
- Having Grandma and Grandpa nearby.

Be determined to give thanks. Be determined to be a wife or mother with a good attitude.

Every day, Lord, I want to give thanks,
to praise and glorify Your name.

Read 1 Thessalonians 5

In Quiet Days

And whatsoever ye do, do it heartily, as to the Lord,
and not unto men. –Colossians 3:23

Our Sunday school lesson was the timeless, familiar story of Queen Esther. In a dark time of need for the Jews, Esther put her life on the line to present her case to her husband, the king in a brilliant show of tact and diplomacy.

We know that story. We stand in awe at her courage and how she appealed to her uncle to request all the Jews in the city of Shushan to fast and pray for her. She and her maidens also fasted.

Esther was not called to come to the King for thirty days. I wonder about the kind of life she lived. Was she lonely? How many years were given to her? Did she have meaningful things to do?

What we know about Queen Esther only covers a few days in the years she lived. Take time to refresh your memory by reading the book of Esther. After reading, consider: how can we live life well? Can we live life well only when we love the Lord with all our hearts and seek His approval above all else?

Not many of us are called to prominent places and have big things to do for God. Could our opinions about what is big in life be faulty? I believe one of the bigger things God gave me to do was to be a mother and raise children for Jesus. Faithfulness in small things at home is paramount. Faithfulness to whatever task God gives is a big thing.

Day after day, many women work in the quietness (or not-so-quiet) of their homes. They faithfully teach and train children for Jesus. They do work that is often unnoticed or even unappreciated.

119

Who notices if a mother keeps her house well? Who sees if she spends time to teach her children obedience and kindness? Who gives commendation to a woman for doing what needs to be done?

God bless the men who thank their wives for ordinary work well done. God bless the women who are willing to do their work "as to the Lord."

Can we live life well only when we love the Lord with all our hearts and seek His approval above all else?

Most of Esther's days are not recorded for the world to see and know. I wonder if she had not been faithful in the quiet days, would she have stood the test of doing what she could for the Lord in the public places?

In the quiet days and the quiet places, Lord, where
no one sees or knows but You, may all I do
bring Your honor and praise.

Read Colossians 3

Snapshots
of Kenya

I will therefore that the younger women marry, bear children, guide the house, give none occasion to the adversary to speak reproachfully. –1 Timothy 5:14

A friend in missions shared this teachable moment:

I was telling my ten- and fourteen-year-old sons today they need to be dependable and do their jobs so well that people say, "When I want something done properly, I call one of their boys."

Do you know what my ten-year-old charmer said? "But mom, if you're like that people will always want you to work and who wants to work all the time?"

"Son," I said, "That is being a slacker and those who don't work don't eat. Do you want to grow up eating out of trash cans?"

He momentarily got dreamy eyed while contemplating the option of that as opposed to real work. The older ones were snickering in the background. I snickered too.

"I hate these rats in Kenya," my friend went on to share. "I was touching up the children's mopping job before I went to bed last night. A rat ran out from under the stove and disappeared toward our garage. I hate rats. I need to get up early and do laundry. What if I see a rat? I'm believing that God cares about small details like that and asking Him that the rat would eat the bait my husband scattered around and die."

I'm writing down when I see a wife respond in an exceptionally nice way to her husband, especially when I know a nice response might not be easy. I don't see it often, but when I do, it's good to take note because that's how I want to be. For instance, one lady responded with much patience when her husband asked the same question three or four times (I was beginning to wonder if he was half-deaf).

There is much darkness, but I know that greater is He that is in us than He that is in the world (1 John 4:4).

When we visited a village church in the country, Bentor was the Sunday school teacher. I was encouraged by her life of faithfulness to Jesus, even though her husband is not living for Jesus. That blessed me.

I went with my husband to visit a woman in the community. Her daughter has had five children she deserted, and the daughter's mother cares for them. One month ago, the daughter had another baby. When the baby was three days old, the daughter was already tired of the baby and threw him down the *choo* (outhouse hole), where he was rescued four hours later. This is so sad, and as mama Sara told me, he's only one among many.

There is much darkness, but I know that greater is He that is in us than He that is in the world (1 John 4:4).

God cares about all areas of our life.

There is so much ordinary work on the mission field, God. Help me to work cheerfully, and to not be so particular that I neglect what is most important.

Read Deuteronomy 6

One Drumstick

Given to hospitality. –1 Timothy 3:2

"Mom, I invited five friends for Sunday lunch. If you are not here, I will cook," a text from my adult son read. We were traveling home from a wedding. We had left at nine that morning and it was nearing nine at night. On Friday evening, we had had guests—eight children and two couples. Now, would I be okay with company again? I replied that I would be at home and would add rice and beans and chicken to my menu.

"You could make some brownies," I suggested, "or we can have ice cream for dessert." He did not feel like leaving his studies, though he did cut cheese chunks for me. I got another text: "Can two more guys come?"

Hospitality is a ministry for Him who loves all people.

I have learned over the years to keep it simple. Many people come through our doors. I cooked a big kettle of rice and beans. I cut up more chicken. I would serve green beans, applesauce, and two big packs of dinner rolls.

When Mark and I drove in after church, our lane was full of vehicles. How many people had come? My son met me on the porch. "Mom, two more girls came." God gave me calmness. If the food reached, great. If not, there were plenty of other things to eat.

We added another leaf to our table and met new people from various church groups.

Mark asked everyone to share about themselves and a quirk from their lives. Conversation flowed around the table. This group had traveled. There was laughter and raised eyebrows at some of the amazing stories.

Ashly was entertaining. She came to Jesus through a kid's ministry. Laughter and giggles just flowed from her like a fountain. Randy asked if her family was Christian? She bubbled with laughter at the question and remarked that she is the only one.

Caleb was tall, a heavily-bearded young man. When we met at the door, I remarked to him that with such a name I hoped he was a man of God. A Canadian lady was studying to become a registered nurse.

The food disappeared. My son served coffee with the ice cream. I took up the leftovers: one drumstick, a cup or two of rice, a handful of green beans. Everyone was happy and fed.

That morning I had read that we should cheerfully share our homes with those who need a meal or a place to stay (1 Pet. 4:9). I welcome our children's friends into our home. This, too, is for Jesus.

Hospitality is a ministry for Him who loves all people.

Jesus, taking time for people gives me joy,
and at times much work. Strengthen me.

Read 1 Peter 4

Singing on
the Couch

I will bless the LORD *at all times: his praise shall
continually be in my mouth.* –Psalm 34:1

“**O**n days when the morning is not going well, I love to call my children to sing with me on the sofa,” shared one mom. Though she is not an accomplished singer, she chooses to bless the Lord in that way. Her children love it when she calls them to sing. Their whiny attitudes disappear as they praise God in song. She remembers her three-year-old son standing straight and tall, directing with joy on his face. She fondly remembers those times, especially because the days with her only son are gone. Today he is singing in heaven's choir.

Gather your children around you and sing His praises.

Singing creates a spirit of oneness and bonds people together. This mother chooses to bless the Lord at all times, not because of the circumstances she is experiencing, but because of who God is to her. She encourages others by sharing, “I am serving Christ when I care for my family and children.”

Here is an idea to cure the grouchiness in your heart and in your home. Gather your children around you and sing His praises.

How many times does the enemy tempt mothers with wishful

thoughts of being able to do other things? Women can influence each child in each family for Jesus.

Ideas to squelch grouchiness:

- Memorize scriptures. Children love bedtime attention. Post verses by their bed and go over them each night.
- Sing together when you tuck them in.
- Linger and tell a Bible story, or a story of your own. They love hearing about when mom and dad were small.
- Pray together; teach them to give their fears to Jesus.
- Teach them that God is awake.
- Have a song for the month.
- Visit a nursing home or an elderly person; sing songs and recite verses there.
- Help them think of others, a note for the preacher, a gift for the Sunday school teacher.
- Teach children to give, not just feel entitled to receive gifts.

Life is fragile. The days and years go by swiftly on the wings of time. Cherish the days with your small children.

My Father in heaven, I want to
find joy in each season of life.

Read Luke 6:1-38

Yes Woman

The LORD will perfect that which concerneth me:
thy mercy O LORD, endureth forever: forsake not the
works of thine own hands. –Psalm 138:8

"Here's a real-life example of being a Yes Woman [one who is cheerful with her husband's plans]," my friend shared:

We stopped at one of these new hip-hop malls in Nairobi. It's a beautiful place. It was refreshing to walk around and look at all the glitz and glamor and soak up the beautiful landscape of the Kenya I love. It's nice to actually go somewhere and sit on green grass by lovely flowers and not have to frame any responses to requests for an hour or so. I had browsed in the bookshop looking for a coffee table book to give our schoolteacher as a gift. She cleaned the offices for the last two years but was ready for a break now.

And there suddenly I saw, in the midst of all the crowd of happy shoppers, all my chilluns all easy to pick out. They were beaming smiles and happy, riding Segways and little remote controlled four wheelers. My first response was to ask why . . . and how? My husband told me that we needed to be extra careful with our spending this month because of extra stateside expenses. (Too often lately my response would be to ask about it then and there, questioning if he's sure we can do this . . . Blah, blah, nag, nag.) Instead, when my fourteen-year-old son zoomed by on his Segway and told me that they bargained for the price of twenty dollars for twenty minutes for six children to zoom around, I just smiled and kept my trap shut.

In the grand scheme of life, a dad who treats his children indulgently on family day is going to be much more upbuilding to a family than a shrewish mom who poured cold water on all the fun and her husband.

> *May your life put the light of happiness in your husband's and children's eyes.*

Let your husband lead. Work at being a yes woman, a happy woman. Say yes when given short notice. "Do you want to come with me?" "Yes" to satisfying him. "Yes" and "Thank you" when he brings an expensive item home that you may feel is too lavish. Don't pour cold water on his ideas. Stand beside him and make him proud that you are his wife.

May your life put the light of happiness in your husband's and children's eyes.

Lord, help my life to put the light of happiness in my husband's and children's eyes.

Read Psalms 127 and 128

God My Refuge

Cast thy burden upon the LORD, and he shall sustain thee.
–Psalm 55:22

I know I need to keep growing and really believing that God is my refuge. When I am troubled about situations, something that helps me is pouring my heart out to God in written prayers. Sometimes my writing includes tears. God sees my tears. The psalmist mentions our tears being in God's bottle. Does He tenderly collect them when they run off our faces?

When I am really troubled, I sometimes just sit and read chapter after chapter in the Bible, especially the Psalms. Isaiah 53 is another chapter that ministers to me. Here Isaiah says that Jesus has borne our griefs and carried our sorrows. Reading this prophet's words helps us form a picture of that in our mind, which helps us to remember that we are not alone. God carries our burden. Often, it seems I need to give some burdens to God again and again.

Mothers go through many changes. A young woman has adjustments with every child added to the family. Her body goes through changes; her emotions fluctuate. There is nothing like parenting to make us realize how much we need God's help.

Older women experience huge changes with each child that leaves the home. There are changes with every wedding and with menopause. I want God to be my daily refuge and strength. I do not want to depend only on my husband and children to feel needed, wanted, and loved.

Seasons of Life

"It seems my children just don't need me so much anymore," Clara confided as we chatted in the greenhouse. This stage of life, when children leave, holds so many changes and is just a big challenge to graciously accept.

My daughter thought it rather unbelievable that I was thinking of the adjustment of planting a garden without children. She was adjusting to planting with three children aged three and under.

I want God to be my daily refuge and strength.

For mothers who work with their children every day, it is a big change when they all have jobs away from home and mom has to even empty the trash cans! My daughters used to be responsible for a meal each week. They cleaned the house, did laundry, and baked and cooked. It's a major shift when daughters leave. I remind myself that this is all in God's good plan.

Whatever your children's age, graciously accept each stage. Live so that the Master may say, "Well done, thou good and faithful servant" (Matt. 25:21).

God longs to be your refuge in every change and every place.

God, I need You to be my refuge in
every change and in every place.

Read Psalm 46

Babies
and Beads

Learn not the way of the heathen. –Jeremiah 10:2

Numerous times in Africa I saw a baby with beads around his neck, his wrists, or his stomach. *Why were those beads on children?* I wondered.

Sharon and her small son came to church. I was surprised to see a silver and red bead bracelet hanging on George's small neck. I asked Sharon about the bracelet, and she said her aunt had bought it for George. It was a charm for protection. The beads did not protect the little toddler from getting burned. They did not protect him from malaria and other illnesses in their household.

One Monday afternoon, I visited Sharon and her aunt. We sat in the shade under their mango tree. I asked questions and told them I wanted to understand African culture. "Why do the children wear beads?"

"In Kenya children die because a spell may be cast on them," she said. "The beads are to protect against such a curse." The darkness and superstitious fears are real in Africa, and these fears are not automatically laid down when people come to Jesus.

We discussed 1 John 4:4, which tells us that we can overcome because God is stronger than Satan. We read verses about trust and God's protection. We read Psalm 34:7 too: "The angel of the LORD encampeth round about them that fear him, and delivereth them."

"Pray for God's protection every day and night," I encouraged them. "Pray and ask God what to do about beads on George."

I cannot tell them what to do. They need to seek, pray, and hear from God themselves. I hope they can believe that God is so much stronger than those who cast spells. God can protect George.

My friend Cynthia, who worked in Ghana and Kenya, once said, "God wants to show Himself strong in our lives. He doesn't need beads or any such thing to solicit His attention. He simply wants our complete trust. There is a need for added prayers to break through the dark strongholds of Africa."

> *"He simply wants our complete trust."*

Is our American culture reverting more and more to pagan practices? What about tattoos, body piercings, and amber necklaces for babies?

After having lived in Kenya, I was surprised to hear of amber bead necklaces used here to help babies in teething, drooling, or to calm them. How can beads have power? Do they have more value than just a costly ornament?

A wise friend said, "Shouldn't we as God's people take the high road by asking the question 'Is it right, good, pure, and upbuilding?' Instead, many people ask, 'What's wrong with it?' or 'What can I get by with?'"

I want to trust Your awesome power, Lord.

Read 1 John 4

Changes
and Tears

Thou tellest my wanderings: put thou my tears into thy
bottle: are they not in thy book? –Psalm 56:8

C hanges and adjustments on the mission field and in other
places we live our lives are not easy. I remember adjusting to
Kenya, and the copious tears I shed. I missed our three oldest children, our first grandchild, and friends at home. Often, I
went into our bedroom and shut the door to cry. Teenage sons are
not so comfortable with their mother's tears. They could always de-
tect when I was struggling, though I tried to
wash the traces of tears from my face. It *God's Word is*
helped when my husband put his arm
around me and was understanding. I was *encouraging*
thankful when he gave me a strong shoulder *and life-giving.*
to cry on.

I wish we were not ashamed of tears. It is
okay to cry. Jesus wept. God created tears as
a release, a normal, healthy way to express emotions. A baby cries
when he needs comfort, food, or support. A baby's cry at birth is a
good signal of health. Adults also need the release that tears bring.

God's Word is encouraging and life-giving. There are thirty-four
verses with the word tears. Study what the Bible says about tears.

- God told Hezekiah, "I have heard thy prayer, I have seen thy tears: behold, I will heal thee" (2 Kin. 20:5).
- "Weeping may endure for a night, but joy cometh in the morning" (Psa. 30:5).
- Jesus wept over Mary and Martha's sorrow (John 11:35). He sees and cares.
- The angel and Jesus said to Mary, "Dear woman, why are you crying?" (John 20:13, 15 NLT).

The Word spoke to my heart. God sees and He cares about our tears. Tears show a tender heart. Tears are healing. We give our tears to our Father. Be thankful you can cry. Tears are good for health. My mother experienced a lot of pain in her family. When she was older, though she loved the Lord, she could no longer shed tears.

Give the hard things to Jesus. Share your feelings with your husband. Open up to a trusted friend on the mission field. Share with someone in church. We are not meant to live alone. We need strength and the encouragement found in the family of God.

God knows. He sees your tears, and He will strengthen and help you. When you see a friend in tears, reach out to comfort and bless. You may not understand, but you can always show love and care.

Thank You, Lord, that You care about everything.
You see my tears and hold me up.

Read John 20

Pleasant
and Green

The righteous shall flourish like the palm tree. –Psalm 92:12

Τhe sight of palm trees refreshes my mind. I have appreciated them in the tropical climates I have called home. A rising full moon framed with swaying palm trees is breathtaking. The palm tree is a symbol of life. Palm trees live long. Their fruit—coconuts, bananas, plantains, and dates—are sweet, and palm leaves are always green.

There is much usefulness in this tree. The leaves are woven into mats; the fibers provide thread and rigging for boats, are used in hats, flooring, hammocks, and wicker furniture. The wood is pressed to extract oils for soft drinks, cooking, and soap. After fermentation, the sap becomes a liquor or vinegar.

What are ways we can flourish as a palm tree?

- By standing firm in the faith.
- With a daily love for and walk with God.
- By having Christian friends who speak into our lives.
- By sincerely desiring to serve Jesus and care about people.

Winds of crazy circumstances will not fell those firmly rooted in Jesus. Compare this to the wicked, who flourish as the grass but soon wither and are cut down.

An eighty-four-year-old man offered devotions in our church

one morning. He read the beatitudes. It was encouraging to hear him share the Word. After church, his wife Susan told me that they were memorizing the beatitudes. I was inspired that at their age they are hiding God's Word in their hearts. Susan remarked that when she cannot sleep at night it is a good thing to quote all the scriptures she knows.

God enables us to be fruitful at every age.

∽

In church one evening, Hosanna pulled a paper out of her Bible and shared thoughts on praise that blessed her in her time with God that morning. I thought that was sweet.

Jeremiah 17:7-8 holds the key for green leaves.

Blessed is the man that trusteth in the LORD, and whose hope the LORD is. For he shall be as a tree planted by the waters, and that spreadeth out her roots by the river, and shall not see when heat cometh, but her leaf shall be green; and shall not be careful in the year of drought, neither shall cease from yielding fruit.

God enables us to be fruitful at every age.

Do I want my life to be refreshing, to be a blessing, to be fruitful for God?

Precious Jesus, guide my days; keep me near You.

Read Psalm 92

Serve My Generation

I have found David the son of Jesse, a man after mine own heart, which shall fulfil all my will. –Acts 13:22

I desire to be a woman who pleases God, embracing His will, loving my husband and children, and doing all I can to serve my generation.

God gives ideas and inspiration for building and serving.

- Take an interest in the older women; share books or things that are dear to your heart.
- Babysit, send them out for supper, pay for their meal.
- Drop in at a friend's house to chat.
- Take an active interest in others' lives, asking about their children in mission work.
- Invite church people over.
- Share garden things, butternut squash or whatever you have.
- Write notes of appreciation.
- Invite single ladies to drive with you to mission services.
- Help young married ladies with canning.

My adult son still remembers a young lady in church who was nice to him. She happily helped us out with babysitting and took an interest in our children. She gave a bunny to our son, brought clothes from a yard sale, and was my friend as well. I was sad when she married a man from another church and left ours.

I have been the recipient of so much love and goodness. When my mother was in hospice care, friends from church ministered to us by bringing in a meal or desserts like fresh cinnamon rolls, or by lending support through care and a listening ear. My sister from out-of-state arrived and took care of mom for a few days. She blessed and supported us with her sweet loving spirit. When my mother passed away, our minister and his wife brought soup and a cheese and meat tray. Neighbors brought food as well.

God gives ideas and inspiration for building and serving.

When we were packing up and getting ready to fly to Kenya, my friend Savannah walked in with her hands full of fresh pumpkin pies, bread, and deviled eggs. She rolled up her sleeves and ironed, packed, and cheerfully helped wherever needed. Ladies from church cleaned our house after we left.

Take time to live out Galatians 6:10: "As we have therefore opportunity, let us do good unto all men, especially unto them who are of the household of faith."

Thank You, Lord, for my wonderful friends
who bring cheer to my days.

Read John 13:33-35

A Daughter's Vigil

Knowing that of the Lord ye shall receive the reward of the inheritance; for ye serve the Lord Christ. –Colossians 3:24

Who can understand the strong ties of love and care between a mother and her daughter? A daughter needs God's wisdom and strength so much when the day comes that roles are reversed and she cares for her mother.

I quietly entered room 2092. Calliope was sleeping soundly. Antonia had dozed off in the bedside chair. I wanted to show my love and support. I remembered the bleakness, the sacrifices, the pain of caring for my mother until God called her home.

We long to do meaningful things in life. We want to do big things for God. Antonia echoed my sentiments that someday it would be rewarding to cook meals for the homeless shelter, or volunteer in the hospital. "We would like to invite more guests to our house," she wistfully told me. "But for now, we cannot because of Mom."

We hope to model for our children what we wish to receive some day.

Antonia and I prayed together by her mother's bedside. We left the hospital together, but her mom did not even know we had been there. She was drugged to calm her restless and irrational behavior. Yet Antonia wanted to be with her, even though she was exhausted. Taking care of a mother who was not a believer, who talked much, and who spewed unkind words was a work for God for my friend.

Taking care of a mother who was battered by life's storms and disappointments, who looked so sad, whose spring of tears were dried up, who lapsed into dementia and silence, was a test to the very core of my being. Yet, we took our mothers to doctors' appointments; we stayed at home and missed events we yearned to attend. We cared for them. We loved them for Jesus. Caring for mothers is not unnoticed by God; it is for a season of life.

We hope to model for our children what we wish to receive some day. Someday God may lead us to love the homeless, to volunteer in a hospital, to host many people, or to be a missionary in a faraway land. Perhaps someday; but for today, we love mother.

The bond of love between mothers and daughters is strong. Caring for them pleases God.

May the care we show at home please You, Lord.

Read 1 Timothy 5

A Big "Praise the Lord"

Ye shall go out with joy, and be led forth with peace.
–Isaiah 55:12

How many times do we pray before we travel and ask God for His protection over us? How many times do we pull into our own driveways safe and sound and remember to thank the Lord?

God is watching over us. He loves and guards us. I know that does not mean accidents never happen to God's children, yet surely, surely, we should praise God for all the times He has kept us safe from harm and danger. God has answered so many prayers.

God is watching over us.

Mark and I were nearly home. We were driving through the little town of Trail in the dusk of twilight. Suddenly I saw two deer crossing the road. "Mark, there are deer!" I emphatically exclaimed. I thought we would hit them, so I squeezed my eyes shut and waited for the impact. Two deer were crossing and the third one coming onto the road.

God made a way. Mark swerved into the other lane, and we passed safely between the second and third deer. It was a close one! I was so relieved. Glancing back, I saw more deer. I am grateful my husband is an excellent driver, and I know God kept us safe!

There was another time God answered our prayers for protection. One afternoon at five o'clock, Micah was driving home from a job with four men in the sturdy work truck. They were crossing a bridge when he felt the truck shake. He glanced in the rearview mirror and saw a tire fly off the truck, and watched as the tire flew up ahead, in front of the truck. As Micah slowed down, he felt a worse jolt. The second tire of the dual wheel flew off and careened ahead of the truck. Micah braked, of course, and the truck shimmied and swayed. He fought the steering wheel, easing up on the brake. It was clear to him that if he braked more, he would lose control. By this point he had crossed over the bridge and had taken his foot off the accelerator. He let the truck slow down on its own. The metal rim was grinding on the pavement, and he had to fight to stay on the road. Finally, the truck slowed to a stop. He put it into four-wheel drive and limped off into a driveway.

Everyone in that truck was grateful that there had not been a terrible accident.

I was overflowing with thankfulness. Thank you Jesus for protecting Micah.

God, how can I praise You enough? You have answered
prayers for protection countless times.

Read Isaiah 55

Barns and Treasures

She will do him good and not evil all the days of her life.
–Proverbs 31:12

My friend challenges me in how she does her best in loving and in making her husband a success in whatever job he chooses to work.

When their children were young, his work was tearing down old barns. They hauled old wood homes, reselling weathered old boards, beams, and cut stones. The work was hard and sometimes dangerous.

Sometimes they traveled from state to state to dismantle old barns in our area. They lived in a motor home and stayed at a campground with their five children. The youngest was three, but I did not hear Regina complain. She and the children helped on the barn sites as they could. She visited friends and even invited us to the campground for a picnic supper. The family took time for fun too, visiting local attractions, especially things relating to nature.

Happy is the man whose wife chooses to love always: supporting, praying for, and accepting her husband.

Today his work is vastly different. He says he is a treasure seeker.

He likes going to yard sales, thrift stores, and book sales, seeking valuable treasures he can buy cheaply and resell online.

This wife supports and blesses her husband by advertising, shipping items, and many other tasks. She needs to be patient with the extra *stuff* (or treasures) in their house. Again, she is grateful. She said she loves being at home with this work and chooses to bless her husband in the best possible way she can. Their two youngest sons work with their dad. Her attitude has blessed their home and leaves a lasting example to her sons and daughters.

In the words of Dorcas Showalter,

True intimacy is knowing, accepting and loving your spouse just the way he is.

If you withhold your love until he changes the way you think he should be, he will never meet your standard, and you will miss out on the great wealth of blessing God has promised to those who obey Him.[8]

Happy is the man whose wife chooses to love always: supporting, praying for, and accepting her husband.

I want to stand by my husband, Lord,
and do what I can to bless him.

Read Proverbs 31

---

[8] Dorcas Showalter, *Flourish* (Harrisonburg, VA: Christian Life Publications, 2020), 38.

Accepted

For he is our peace, who hath made both one, and hath
broken down the middle wall of partition between us.
–Ephesians 2:14

While chatting with a friend from church, I thanked her for loving and accepting everyone in our church. People and families are different from one another and some have a hard time fitting into our church families. My friend confided that she is accepting because at one time, when living in a different place, she did not feel accepted. That painful experience created within her a heart of care. "I just want to accept people." Her acceptance of others has given her good friends today.

May God help us to love people and to love peace.

God's children should be able to show meaningful love and care to people from different background and cultures. Sadly though, sometimes we don't do well in loving and accepting people from our own cultures.

May God help us to love people and to love peace.

Many issues are not in themselves right or wrong. Let's be gracious and caring and let others experience Jesus's love through us. Sometimes that includes trying to understand their point of view, not wavering on Biblical truths, but truly caring and not hurtful to others when we disagree on trivialities.

Scripture says that we are accepted in the beloved, accepted in

Jesus, accepted because of His blood and His love. How much godly acceptance do others feel from me? Ask God for ideas and ways to share His love and kindness. Be willing to give time to bless and show care for others, in church and beyond.

In life's seasons . . .
Sometimes I thrive.
Other times I am weary,
Wounded, and sad.
God does not discard me
 when I fail.
Like I pitch plants
 in the greenhouse
 not doing well.
God heals and helps.
He says,
"I am the Lord that healeth."
May I be compassionate
 and caring to those
 who struggle.
Lend a listening ear,
A helping hand,
And offer prayers.

Can we be accepting of others in our differences of personality and tastes?

Jesus, help me to love people and to live in peace.

Read Ephesians 2

Stories

Thou shalt rise up before the hoary head, and honour the face of the old man, and fear thy God: I am the LORD.
–Leviticus 19:32

We were with a group holding a service for the elderly at Walnut Hills Nursing Home. They each had a life; they still do. Years ago, they were young, strong, beautiful, and useful. Emma had the joy of the Lord on her face. She praised God and was grateful, not grumbling.

Working at the doctor's office in Walnut Creek had kept one lady busy for many fulfilling years.

"I had been a nurse for fifty years," Elsie related. "The highlight of my years of nursing was working in East Africa, Liberia for two years. There were so many needs. I did all kinds of things I would never have done in an American hospital. Later, for seventeen years, I was a caregiver for elderly folks." Elsie was happy to give me a glimpse of her days. The cycle of life goes on. Today, Elsie has others caring for her.

A granddaughter shared this about her admirable grandmother.

My grandmother's first activity each morning is to walk brisk prayer miles, praying for children, grandchildren, and those near her heart. She is a lady who gives and gives. If a family has a need, she is the first to take a meal, or offer her help. She still cans vegetables and soups every summer and shares the jars of food. She knows she is only doing her duty and is one of the most selfless women I know. I admire how she lives life with energy, passion, and in ways that bless many.

My mother had dementia in her later years. We were grateful for two single ladies who helped with her care. They loved her, reading scripture and other books to help pass the time in meaningful ways. One evening I walked over to Mom's house. Susie was sitting on the porch swing, her large German Bible in her work-worn hands. I was so blessed with that scene. Susie found comfort and strength in the Word of God. She shared His love with her caregiving.

There is work for God at every age.

Ervin Hershberger, a friend of ours, was helping with church house cleaning. He was humble enough to do lowly tasks like run the vacuum sweeper, even though he had been the principal at Calvary Bible School for many years. While cleaning, he sat down to rest because he did not feel well. Then he fell and passed out. His friends called the squad. Ervin's request was to not try to bring him back if something happened. God called him home that night. He died as he had lived, in service to God.

There is work for God at every age.

I want to be willing to do ordinary work for You, Lord.

Read Isaiah 25

That Monster

There is none like unto the God of Jeshurun, who rideth upon the heaven in thy help, and in his excellency on the sky. –
Deuteronomy 33:26

Returning to Kenya after our furlough and a son's wedding was difficult. One son was staying in Ohio. One went to Calvary Bible School. Our youngest went back with us. Our family was scattered.

Fatigue haunted us, and discouragement filled our heads. It took a week until we could sleep normally. Jet lag is a dark monster. When I sleep well, I cope better and feel happier about life. It was difficult for my son with us in Kenya. There were many things he liked to do at home in Ohio. He keenly missed his brothers. There were not enough meaningful things to do for an energetic youth at our mission post. That had been a struggle ever since we were in Kenya. On top of everything else, he got sick of doing schoolwork alone.

I want, I need, a stronger faith, which is the belief and trust that God will see us through.

How would I survive if I could not cry out to God? My mind goes to the song phrase: "Abide with me, fast falls the eventide, the darkness deepens, Lord with me abide; When other helpers fail and comforts flee, Help of the helpless, O abide with me."⁹ We desperately needed the shield of faith to quench the fiery darts of the wicked.

Why was I awake so late at night? A drunk man hollered on the road. What an eerie sound he made. Our dog, Roxy, growled and barked. Too many things were disturbing my sleep: a whining mosquito in our net, cats fighting, music from wakes, and Roxy barking yet again.

Will I look for sunshine?

- I was encouraged when my son came and gave me a hug Sunday morning. He thanked me for the note last night. I had acknowledged to him that life feels hard.
- Neighbor Morris handed seven tomatoes to me across the yard fence.
- Mark and I went on a walk and had heart connections. I asked him if he liked it here in Kenya. "I believe it's God's plan for us," he replied.
- He then asked if I liked Kenya. "I am trying," I responded.
- When Dishon visits, he lights up our home with his happiness and gratefulness. One Sunday afternoon I sat beside the hammock where he was resting, and he told me about a robbery. I took notes and wrote a story. Dishon is special to all of us. Our relationship with him makes days in Africa more meaningful.

I want, I need, a stronger faith, which is the belief and trust that God will see us through. I love our quiet evenings at home. We read good books; we sing and are refreshed. I choose to believe and hold onto the promises in the Word. I must pray and commit our lives to God again and again. I believe the promise that God, who rides upon the heavens, is helping me. And finally, I am grateful when the monster jet lag is past and we are rested and revived.

Jesus, help me to find the sunshine in dreary days.

Read Exodus 23:20-30

---

⁹ Henry F. Lyte (1793-1847). Public domain.

Small Prayers,
A Big God

Out of the depths have I cried unto thee, O LORD.
Lord, hear my voice: let thine ears be attentive
to the voice of my supplications. –Psalm 130:1-2

"We cannot find a place that is just right for us to buy," Antonia moaned to a neighbor.

"Well," Roberta told her, "I will pray that you will be able to find a place that is right for you."

Eventually our friends found a place they liked in a quiet neighborhood they wanted.

God is so great. He rules the universe. He knows. He sees all the poverty. He is aware of all the people who are lonely. The ill. The hungry. The starving. Refugees. God is never taken by surprise. How can it be that God is interested and even cares about mundane details in our days, when the world is full of weighty, horrible problems? That is part of the greatness of God that I cannot understand.

"I lost my Birkenstock's," Antonia told Markus. "I guess I will just have to shell out the money to buy another pair." Markus asked her if she had prayed about it? She wondered if lost sandals were too small to pray about. She prayed and that same evening she was amazed to find her favorite sandals in their vehicle.

My son went to an auction on a cold wintery day. After locking his vehicle, he went into the office to get a bidding number. With bidding number in hand, he went back to his car, reached into his coat pocket for his car keys . . . The pocket was empty. He went back to his car. His heart sank to find it locked. What should he do?

How can it be that God is interested and even cares about mundane details in our days, when the world is full of weighty, horrible problems?

⁓

He prayed and asked God to help him find his keys.

A man sitting in a nearby red truck saw Markus as he searched the ground for the keys. He rolled down his window and told him he had found a set of keys behind his truck and was planning to turn them in at the office. My son rejoiced over this quick answer to prayer.

God is so big, so powerful. He is too caring for us to grasp. We cannot wrap our minds around His care. His eyes search through the earth to show Himself strong on behalf of His children.

May we fall on our knees to worship and give thanks through the answers and through the waiting.

Thank You Father that You are all knowing and most powerful. I trust You with my days.

Read 2 Chronicles 16

Shriveled

For his anger endureth but for a moment;
in his favour is life: weeping may endure for a night,
but joy cometh in the morning. –Psalm 30:5

I forgot to give away some of my calla lily bulbs before we flew to Kenya. They sat in the darkness of our basement for over a thousand days. When we returned, I decided to plant them, thinking there might still be life in those dry-looking bulbs. I planted them in an old enamel bowl in the corner of our warm greenhouse. Then one day, I saw a fresh green sprout poking through the soil. I rejoiced. Later there would be speckled green leaves and a lovely white bloom.

I wonder what God is trying to teach me through difficult, dry, and dark seasons of my life?

I wonder what God is trying to teach me through difficult, dry, and dark seasons of my life?

My mind went to Joseph and the lonely years he spent in prison. That was a dismal place of darkness, yet Joseph did not give up. Even in prison, he was faithful. He noticed others and cared about them. In His own time, God brought him out of the dungeon.

I thought of other Bible characters: Moses, Jeremiah, Paul . . . They walked with God, and they obeyed God. They were in the will of God, but that was no guarantee that life would be easy.

Life just is not an easy street. They had severe trials, even though they were faithfully following and obeying God.

A friend of mine in missions was wounded and weary with difficult relationships. "I do pray for you," I told her. "In the darkness of disapproval you are feeling from others, may you feel the light of God's love and never give up hope. Also remember that there are MANY who love you and your family, me included."

I want to believe that God can work beauty out of the difficulties, even as beautiful white lilies bloomed out of my dry shriveled calla lily bulbs.

Why are there difficult, dry seasons in life and relationships? For now, only God knows. Will I trust Him and love? I want to believe that God can work beauty out of the difficulties, even as beautiful white lilies bloomed out of my dry shriveled calla lily bulbs.

I don't want to become dry and shriveled. Through disappointments and difficulties, I want a fresh green shoot of faith and hope thriving in my heart, and reaching up to the light, love, and warmth of God.

God, when I plant seeds, I wait in hope for new growth.
Through the dry, dark seasons I believe
something good is growing.

Read Genesis 39

Washed My Feet

Be kindly affectioned one to another with brotherly love;
in honour preferring one another. –Romans 12:10

When a friend visited our church years ago, she commented that our closed communion was always hard on her. She wished to participate in communion and to wash feet together.

While we were in Africa, that family joined our church. At our first communion service after our return, she said, "I want to wash your feet." She waited for me in the entrance, so we could sit together. I was reeling with culture shock and re-entry into the United States. Her love to me was a balm to my heart.

She remarked, "If we wash each other's feet in church, but do not serve each other outside of church, is it all in vain?"

How do we wash each other's feet outside of church? Can we care about, take time for, and help sisters in church? Footwashing shows that we are all on the same level in the eyes of God. Over the years, this family has washed our feet in meaningful ways. They visited and supported us when we cared for my mother. They attended our children's baptisms and graduations. They traveled miles to my mother's funeral. They were so excited when our daughters got married.

Brighten My Day

It's a good thing to share blessings with friends by phone, text, etc. "A man who returned a van he rented walked in with a box of Coblentz chocolates for me!" Antonia shared. Freedom Hills staff rent vans from them. That family reaches out to customers by sharing coffee, or at times even a meal. One lady from Freedom Hills staff offered to stay with her mom while they attended a funeral in New Jersey. Antonia did not have to look for anyone. God sent that kind offer from someone she knew and trusted.

"Ladies at a luncheon were sharing about who influenced their lives," my friend Cynthia told me. "Many of them were saying, 'My mother was a big influence to me.' I shared your name. You have been a positive in my life, especially in mothering." Those words ministered to my heart, which was hurting due to some difficult struggles I was walking through.

Can we learn to be above average in generosity and kindness?

In the evening of the same day, a thoughtful neighbor gave me a fresh loaf of her delicious sourdough bread.

Can we learn to be above average in generosity and kindness?

I need Your ideas, Lord, on ways to show love and care.

Read John 13

Walking
on Water

*But when they saw him walking upon the sea, they supposed
it had been a spirit, and cried out.* –Mark 6:49

My two-year-old grandson was at a friend's house. His mother returned and found him in a different outfit. He had managed to fall into the creek. Her friend said Adryan was "stepping high" and just walked right into the water. She thought he went in on purpose. We asked him about it. He said, "Adryan cry."

His favorite Bible story is the story of Jesus walking on the water. My daughter thinks that's what Adryan was trying to do. He wanted to walk on the water like Jesus. After they were talking about this, Adryan said, "No, Adryan not walk on water." Now he tells us that Jesus can walk on water, but Adryan cannot. I praise God for His protection over my grandson that day.

When Jesus came into the ship, the wild winds stopped.

The account of Jesus walking on the water is found in Matthew, Mark, and John. The disciples were having difficulty rowing on a wild dark sea. When they saw Jesus walking on the water, they were troubled and thought it was a spirit. They cried out in fear. Jesus called out to them, "Be of good cheer: It is I; be not afraid" (Mark 6:50). When Jesus came into the ship, the wild winds stopped. They that were in the ship came and worshiped Him, saying, "Of a truth thou art the Son of God" (Matt. 14:33).

In the wild winds of my life, will I come to Jesus?

COME

Lord, I'm on a turbulent sea,
Oh, Father bid me come to Thee.
The waves are dark, foreboding, near,
But You call, come, be of good cheer.
To Thee, oh Lord, I stretch my hand.
Forever guide me in this land,
To do Your will my heart's desire,
Oh fill me with Your holy fire.
Serving, giving my all for Thee,
Oh Lord, to none else will I flee,
Doing Your work, loving Your will,
My yearning heart You love and fill.
Each day You call, "Come to me,"
A gracious servant let me be.
I come to kneel before Your throne,
Oh, make my life always Your own.

> *You protected my grandson, Father.*
> *Thank You, thank You, thank You.*

Read Matthew 14:22-36

Long Visits

Be ye also patient; stablish your hearts:
for the coming of the Lord draweth nigh. –James 5:8

Visits in Africa take a long time. Sweet Maria, a kindhearted widow, was our first stop one morning. Her small hut's earthen floor was swept impeccably clean, and crocheted doilies were placed on her chairs. After welcoming us inside, we stood for prayer, then she went outside to make chai.

Thick leafy green boughs of a mango tree comprised the roof of her outdoor kitchen among large rocks. A small fire of burning sticks crackled merrily under her kettle which sat on three stones. She was delighted to serve us hot chai and groundnuts (peanuts), which she raised in her garden. I was delighted with the wholesome food.

These visits last a long time, so we need to be patient. Their hospitality and generosity are outstanding. They want to serve food to guests. One cannot just sit and chat and then leave thirty minutes later. We must wait for the chai to heat and for other food to be set out: bread, *mandazis*, or whatever is handy for the host to serve that day. Time with Maria was important.

Visiting the Africans in their homes helps us learn to know them like nothing else does. Again Maria went outside, this time to share cups of chai with her grandchildren.

Finally, she came back in and happily shared a lengthy testimony. She related, "On a day long ago I was in a boat fishing on a lake with some others. A huge hippo overturned our boat, and others came to help us. We were all saved. God saved each and every one of us."

On one of our first visits to Maria's house, she came in with a pretty brown hen in her arms. She tied the hen to a table leg and informed us that it was a gift for us to take home. The hen hungrily pecked up the kernels of corn Maria threw to her. She would not send her gift or her guests away hungry. I was awestruck at the Africans' generosity. It would be rude, a breach of culture, to refuse their gifts.

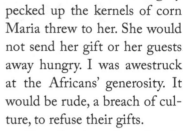

Visiting the Africans in their homes helps us learn to know them like nothing else does.

One Sunday after church, Samson drove with us to Maria's house. I brought a kettle of cooked chicken and a pan of banana bread. Maria stirred up a steaming pot of *ugali* (cornmeal added to boiling water until it is thick enough to slice). We enjoyed the time together over a feast of foods.

Maria loves to sing. On many occasions we sang with her in her small tidy hut. She would give us her chairs while she sat on a small bench against the wall with two little grandsons squeezed tightly beside her.

Singing was a wonderful connection with Kenyan friends. Love is spelled *time*.

Lord, help me to learn from this culture's example of taking time to sit and visit and to be generous with food.

Read Genesis 18:1-19

Write an E-Mail

*I thank my God upon every remembrance of you, Always in
every prayer of mine for you all making request with joy.*
–Philippians 1:3-4

You can truly bless missionaries by praying for them. *Prayer
is big.* Letting them know you are praying for them is a
work for the Lord. Encourage missionaries by praying and
taking time to write them an e-mail or a letter.

I complained to my daughters that I had sent more than one
hundred emails about life in Kenya to my
friends and church group. I received one re-
ply. My daughter responded, "Too bad. You
know, Mom, friends of ours went to mission
training in New York before going to Thailand
and were told that if missionaries want to stay
connected to their church, they have to be the
ones who take the time to pursue it. Lack of response is fairly normal, even though it shouldn't be that way."

*Jesus is my
treasure.*

On another evening I sent an e-mail from Kenya to my six-
ty-person friends group. The next morning I had received ten re-
plies. That was an unusual, amazing, and encouraging response.

I was tempted by those e-mails. I was curious what they said.
Thankfully, I went first to the Word. Zechariah 1 and 2 spoke to
my heart, telling me to turn to the Lord. I find it meaningful to
write prayers about what God tells me in the Word. This morning I
wrote: "Lord, I praise you for the wall of fire You are around me for

protection. You are the glory in my midst. I want to sing and rejoice more and more. You dwell with me."

I need to check my heart. What do I love the most—the Word of God, or e-mails from my friends and children? My goal is to read the Word in the morning before I check my technology. It is a way I strive to honor God.

My heart sings:

We worship and adore You,
Bowing down before You,
Songs of praises singing,
Hallelujahs ringing,
Hallelujah, hallelujah,
Hallelujah! Amen. (Author unknown)

There are many earthly treasures to lure and draw my heart and soul away from God. Jesus is my treasure.

I need friends too. I pored over those ten emails and was encouraged.

Jesus, You are my dearest treasure. I treasure time with You.
I treasure my friends. Thank You for so many blessings.

Read Deuteronomy 30

My Hard Heart

Then shall he answer them, saying, Verily I say unto you,
Inasmuch as ye did it not to one of the least of these,
ye did it not to me. –Matthew 25:45

hile vacationing in Mombasa, a lovely coastal town with palm trees, beaches, and white sand, I glanced into a touristy shop. What an array of pretty African handcrafts greeted me! My next stop was a modern grocery store.

Then my heart sank when I saw a poor crippled woman on the sidewalk, sitting in front of the store. I did not stop to offer a kind word and a coin to the poor woman with an extremely difficult life. I brushed past her and went in to buy groceries for our family. More food for us. We, who are wealthy compared to many in this land. My conscience pricked me. I got a coin out of my purse ready to give to her when we were done shopping. I came out of the store and glanced around, but my heart sank . . . the crippled lady was gone.

Africa has so many crippled people. There are people who get around by dragging their bodies along, using their hands to propel themselves forward because their legs are not functional. There are many with huge tumors on their heads, on their stomachs, or elsewhere. I have seen large goiters on necks. There are adults and children who are lame and use a stick to support themselves as they walk.

One morning, a crippled woman, supporting herself with a stout stick, shuffled into church. She sat beside a mission lady who smiled a friendly welcome. The newcomer was unkempt, unwashed, so she smelled badly. The mission lady was glad for the restless child on her lap so she could make an exit.

One morning we were at Lake Victoria for a picnic breakfast. As we were getting into the old gray cruiser to leave, a man came to our window and pulled up his shirt to display a huge tumor.

God, forgive me. Help me to show compassion and love somehow.

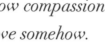

What can we do? I am weary of seeing such things.

God, forgive me. Help me to show compassion and love somehow. To not just look the other way. To not purposely avoid the pleading cripples. I can give a kind word. I can give coins.

O Lord, forgive my hard heart.
Fill me with your love and kindness.

Read Matthew 25:31-46

My Neighbor

But he, willing to justify himself, said unto Jesus,
And who is my neighbor? –Luke 10:29

A stylish lady who spoke English well came to our gate one day. It was comforting to converse with her in my mother tongue. She asked if she could have a Bible storybook for her daughter. I enjoyed getting to know her. I liked visiting her, her mother-in-law, and daughters at their nearby hut. I spoke English; she interpreted in Luo for the aged mother-in-law. We sang Luo and English songs together. We chatted at the market. It was good to have friends in the neighborhood.

A few months later, she was ill. I wondered what was wrong with her health. Africans do not lightly admit they have AIDS, not even when they are dying. There is still such a stigma against AIDS. God, why? Why can't she live? She has two small daughters, Irene and Idah. Don't they need a mom? She was reaping a horrible harvest for her choices and her lifestyle. Why must there be more orphans in Kenya? Did she give up hope when her husband took a second wife? Why did she not get medical treatment? She could have gotten free treatment before it was too late, but her health continued to regress. We took time to visit her in two different hospitals and in her home numerous times. I took food for her.

One day in her house, she was curled up on her bed. She was literally wasting away. Once strong and beautiful, she was now pathetically thin. Her twelve-year-old daughter was attending her. What could I say? I reached in my bag for the Word of God. I opened my Bible, and God led me to Psalm 25. I read: "Look upon my affliction and my pain; and forgive all my sins." The words were so meaningful. I asked Jacklyn, "Do you want to pray that prayer?" The sick woman nodded and repeated after me, "Look upon mine affliction and my pain; and forgive all my sins." Her young daughter, behind her, seriously mouthed the same words. I thought of the dying thief on the cross who asked Jesus to remember him when He went into His kingdom.

This world and all people in it are groaning—groaning in travail until God will say that time will be no more.

The last time I saw Jacklyn, she was so weak it took a great effort to sit up. One morning they transported her to a hospital out of the area. The next time I saw her, she was in her coffin. Death is so cold, so still. Her daughters and friends were weeping and wailing.

God's moral laws were designed to keep people from prostitution and sickness. This world and all people in it are groaning—groaning in travail until God will say that time will be no more.

Oh God, hearing about AIDS and knowing
people with AIDS are two different things.
Show me how to be a neighbor.

Read Luke 10:25-37

Called to Love

Beloved, let us love one another: for love is of God;
and every one that loveth is born of God, and knoweth God.
−1 John 4:7

P eople sometimes say, "We can't trust the Africans." I ask this: are Americans all trustworthy? Does not God call us to love all people?

Susan[10] was a nineteen-year-old single mom in Kenya who I spent a lot of time with. I first met her at a Bible study. She was pregnant and had moved from the city to a relative's house to have her baby.

I loved spending time with Susan. She spoke English fluently, and I found it fun to connect with a Kenyan in my mother tongue. We sang together and pored over scripture. I shared books with her. She memorized verses. When we needed an interpreter, we would ask Sharon to go with us when we visited her area. She was an educated, pleasant young lady and taught me much about Kenyan culture.

One day she walked out of my life. She left with a neighbor boy and moved away to another town. I don't know if I will ever see her again. Where is Susan? The last time I visited her, little Gregory had a fit. He fell down on the dirt road and sobbed because I was leaving, and he could not go with me.

I was sad when I learned that she had been lying to her aunt and me the last few weeks. She told me her mother was sick in the hos-

---

[10] Name changed.

pital in Kisumu and she was desperate to go visit her. I am so thankful to God that I did not feel led to give her *pesa* (money). She lived with her aunt, but she left on a day her aunt was away, taking numerous things from her aunt's house with her.

I asked the aunt if they had been quarreling, and she said no.

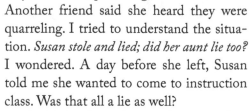

Does not God call us to love all people?

Another friend said she heard they were quarreling. I tried to understand the situation. *Susan stole and lied; did her aunt lie too?* I wondered. A day before she left, Susan told me she wanted to come to instruction class. Was that all a lie as well?

God helped me plant seeds in her life— the seeds of His Word; seeds of care and kindness. What will happen with her? Was the time I spent with her in vain? Only God knows. God knows all things.

I commit it to You, Father, when I plant seeds
and it seems there is no harvest.

Read 1 John 4

All-Night Wake

But the wicked are like the troubled sea, when it cannot rest,
whose waters cast up mire and dirt. There is no peace,
saith my God, to the wicked. –Isaiah 57:20-21

The music was *loud*, pounding, persistent, and demanding. It went on and on through the night. It is a common practice to play music at the all-night Kenyan wakes. The music is not the throbbing from hand-crafted African drums, but recorded music played at high decibels. A generator is rented to enable playing music in country areas with little electricity.

A gentle rain came down the night of the wake, though we could not hear and enjoy it as usually because of the music. I slept fitfully. Every time I awoke, the music was throbbing in my head in the darkness. Normally, I appreciate bird song in the early morning. The birds' melodies are a lovely sound when I awaken; this time it was the loud raucous music that filled my ears.

> *God wants us to worship Him, to be quiet before Him daily.*

Finally, at seven-thirty in the morning, the demanding, depressing music stopped. What a relief.

A verse, Isaiah 30:15, was impressed on my mind. "For thus saith the Lord GOD, the Holy One of Israel; in returning and rest shall ye be saved; In quietness and in confidence shall be your strength: and ye would not."

God is calling us to return to Him, to rest in Him, and to be saved. God wants us to worship Him, to be quiet before Him daily. The choice is ours.

- "But let it be the hidden man of the heart, in that which is not corruptible, even the ornament of a meek and quiet spirit, which is in the sight of God of great price" (1 Pet. 3:4).
- "But whoso hearkeneth unto me shall dwell safely, and shall be quiet from fear of evil" (Prov. 1:33).
- "Better is an handful with quietness, than both the hands full with travail and vexation of spirit" (Eccl. 4:6).
- Pray "that we may lead a quiet and peaceable life in all godliness and honesty" (1 Tim. 2:2).

I want a heart that is quiet before God. The opposite is to be fretful, restless, and worried. I want to grow in trust and quietness.

Jesus, thank You for Your rest and peace in daily life
and in troubled times; You are with me.

Read 1 Timothy 2

Why Did
He Weep?

*Mine eye runneth down with rivers of water for the
destruction of the daughter of my people.*
–Lamentations 3:48

J eremiah is called the weeping prophet. But why did he weep?
Again and again, Jeremiah warned the children of Israel to
repent and turn to God. He warned them of the destruction
and devastation that would come if they did not obey and follow
God. The hearts of the people, however, were hard and their ears
deaf.

Jeremiah was right about the coming destruction, and he wept
because the city was destroyed, the city that was called the perfection of beauty, the joy of the whole earth. The magnificent temple
and the city were burned and lay in smoldering ashes.

Jeremiah said:

- "For these things I weep; mine eye, mine eye runneth down
  with water" (Lam. 1:16).
- "Mine eyes do fail with tears" (Lam. 2:11).
- "Let tears run down like a river day and night" (Lam. 2:18).
- "Mine eye runneth down with rivers of water for the de-
  struction of the daughter of my people" (Lam. 3:48).

In the midst of all his tears, Jeremiah remembered God. In

Lamentations 3:22-25, we find that in the midst of Jeremiah's sorrow, God gave him words of comfort and hope.

It is of the LORD's mercies that we are not consumed, because his compassions fail not. They are new every morning: great is thy faithfulness. The LORD is my portion, saith my soul; therefore will I hope in him. The LORD is good unto them that wait for him, to the soul that seeketh him.

The Lord is good to those who depend on Him, to those who search for Him.

Jeremiah reminded himself that the Lord was his inheritance.

I too will choose to hope in Him. The Lord is good to those who depend on Him, to those who search for Him. It is good to wait quietly for salvation from the Lord.

Everyone's life has struggles and trials. We weep, we cry, and we wonder *why*. Will we throw up our hands in despair? Or will we, like Jeremiah, hold on to the promises, love, mercy, and faithfulness of God Almighty?

It is good to wait quietly for salvation from the Lord.

Waiting is not easy, Lord. I choose to hope and trust in You.

Read Lamentations 3:40-66

Burnout

And he said unto them, Come ye yourselves apart into a desert place, and rest awhile: for there were many coming and going, and they had no leisure so much as to eat.
–Mark 6:31

My friend at a city mission and I were discussing what can be done to prevent burnout.

The Merriam Webster online dictionary states: "Burnout: a condition of someone who has become very physically and emotionally tired after doing a difficult job for a long time. The exhaustion of physical or emotional strength or motivation, usually as a result of prolonged stress or frustration."

She and her husband realize the importance of heart connections for husband and wife. Periodically, they go on dates. Her husband is considerate of her workload. Their six children require a lot of time and energy to care for well. On Tuesday nights, he takes the family and goes for groceries. She recharges with time alone with God, time to pray and time to read. Some nights she loves to spend that time with a friend. (I encouraged her to be grateful. Not every man is that considerate.)

Remember, God wants your heart first of all, most of all.

In Kenya, I often went with Mark to visit church people or other friends. When I was just feeling too tired, I needed to spend time at home. I needed more quietness with God. There was no need to feel guilty about an afternoon nap. When I was resting, my son who was finishing high school at home took care of callers to protect his mother.

These are activities that helped me cope:

- Morning time with God, with the Word and prayer, was a must.
- Enjoying the beauty of nature, God's creations, in a tropical land lifted my spirits. I liked the colorful birds, the unusual plants and flowers.
- Taking time to plant trees and flowers and enjoy them is something I've been refreshed with everywhere we have lived.
- Appreciating the good things about the African culture helped my head. The people truly were generous.
- We loved their native songs and sang with them.
- Sharing my struggles with close missionary women friends helped. I learned I was not alone. We strengthened each other in the Lord.
- Vacations were rejuvenating. Time away from duties and people renewed us.
- Mission work can be hard on a marriage. A couple needs to be intentional about time together and sharing personally the discouragements and joys.

Remember, God wants your heart first of all, most of all. Be quiet before God. Out of that love can come an overflow of service for Him.

I am pleading, Lord, for more rest, more trust
when life is hard and I am weary.

Read Mark 1:35-45

Oh Mary Don't You Weep

Weeping may endure for a night,
but joy cometh in the morning. –Psalm 30:5

Mary Magdalene was weeping at the tomb of Jesus. Two angels in white kindly asked her why she was weeping. Later Jesus also asked her, "Why weepest thou?" (John 20:15).

God sees our tears. He cares.

Why do we weep? We weep when a loved one dies. We weep through life's many changes. I have shed tears each time one of my children left home. I know we didn't raise them for ourselves, and their leaving is in God's good plan. I know they will walk out of our doors. Yet, I weep.

Adjustments in Africa were huge to me. I wept because I could not see my first small grandson for nearly two years. I wanted to go home and help my oldest daughter when her second child was born. I shed tears, lost weight, and nearly got sick with longing. God answered our prayers, and I went!

I wept because I missed out on most of my oldest son's dating and got home only weeks before his wedding. My daughter had two miscarriages while I was in Africa. I cried because I was so far away. Later God blessed them with a baby. What rejoicing! Though I did not see him until he was nine months old.

Africa was so different. The church collapsed and relationships were a constant challenge. We had an infestation of bed bugs. I cried in frustration. Not only was I hot and tired, I was lonely for my daughters and friends who knew and understood me.

Moving felt like starting over. I had to form new relationships. There were no old familiar friends, and it took so much time to adapt to African life.

Are tears a blessing? Or are they something to be ashamed of? It is better to weep and cry out to God than to bottle up our emotions? Tears reveal a tender heart. God knows I never want a hard heart. God sees my tears. He cares.

God sees our tears. He cares.

I like Psalm 56:8 in the New Living Translation: "You keep track of all my sorrows. You have collected all my tears in your bottle. You have recorded each one in your book."

There must somehow be a balance. Tears can be cleansing. God desires me to accept and work with new situations. It helped when I shared struggles with caring friends. We are not meant to struggle through life alone.

When I see my friends cry, sweet Jesus, help me to
give what I would long for: an arm around
the shoulder, a question, and a prayer.

Read John 11:1-36

Lose Your Focus

Wilt thou not revive us again: that thy people
may rejoice in thee? –Psalm 85:6

I need more of the shield of faith. The enemy's fiery darts have discouraged me too often. Why are we in Kenya? Witness seems in vain. It's difficult for our sons. We get so tired. Can we make a difference for Jesus for anyone? I miss the rest of our family and our grandsons. I will not see my daughter's baby until December.

I need to remember that the work of God is not without sacrifice. I need more faith. Faith is heartfelt trust in a personal God. Pray for me to grow in faith. (I sent that request to my daughters when we were in Kenya.)

A friend in another mission shared:

> I can sure identify with you in having allowed some fiery darts whiz past my shield of faith. So often Satan would like for me to get a bad attitude about this or that situation or begin to pity myself, and I have to remind myself (or my husband has to remind me) to look at the big picture.
>
> For instance, our newly painted porch is filthy with hand- and footprints (don't ask me how). The floor is dirty all the time in spite of me sweeping it multiple times a day. My potted canna plant is mangled because of getting caught in the jump rope, being pecked at by the chickens, and bruised by curious hands.
>
> The children are often noisy while my baby is trying to

sleep. I could go on and on. Simply put, I was getting frustrated. I had to step back and be reminded that I could use some discipline techniques and put boundaries in place. Then I could have a clean porch with nice plants...and no children.

These children may be our future church leaders. What am I doing to shape their lives in the right direction? I was challenged to try having upbuilding conversations with them and ask good questions. I could even give them some chores like sweeping the porch, instead of enduring their presence and wishing they would leave. That's why we are here, right?! It's amazing how fast I can lose my focus!

Faith is heartfelt trust in a personal God.

God cares about children. He understands our situation. Go forth in faith and trust.

Heavenly Father, You understand everything we are experiencing. We need Your wisdom so much.

Read Psalm 86

I'm Raising Boys

And that from a child thou hast known the holy scriptures, which are able to make thee wise unto salvation through faith which is in Christ Jesus. −2 Timothy 3:15

"Last evening the garden got tilled!" my daughter shared. "Yeah. But I was only able to get one row of onions in before bedtime. This morning I got up around five twenty, but then Adryan needed food right then. Lyndon promptly got up for the day . . . I was only able to get two little rows of taters in before the rain really started. And now it's too wet to continue planting. I guess I'm raising boys first, and then a garden. So it goes. I'm trying to not exhibit too much of the discouraged gardener syndrome."

While your children are small and the clay is pliable, be intentional with your little ones. Take time with them. Teach them the Word of God. Someday they will be men and women. Someday they will be responsible to answer to God for the choices and decisions they make. May God help us teach the fear of the Lord and live the example of a life that honors, obeys, and respects His Word because we love him so much.

His hand gives me comfort and security all through life.

It is so easy to get bogged down in the daily, constant work of parenting. In the years when our children were small, it helped me to record things they did well, funny things, and incidents that put joy in my heart. That writing exercise helped me to look for the good.

One day I wrote: My dear three-year-old was unaccustomed to the darkness of a cabin without electricity, at a place where we were vacationing. During the night when we were all in bed I heard him cry out, "I need a hand." I went over to his bunk, snuggled beside him, and soon he was fast asleep.

It reminded me of how much I need the hand of God when I am afraid. His hand gives me comfort and security all through life.

Oh Lord, I need Your hand.

Read Proverbs 29

Leave Beauty

He hath made every thing beautiful in his time:
also he hath set the world in their heart. –Ecclesiastes 3:11

I planted a bird of paradise plant beside our house in Kenya. When we moved back to the United States, I was sad it had not yet bloomed. Who would have guessed I would ever see its gorgeous flower? Three years later, three of our sons were back in Kenya visiting friends. They went to our old home in Ng'iya and were amazed at how trees and flowers had grown. They snapped pictures for me. The bird of paradise plant shone with bright orange bird-shaped blooms. That certainly blessed my heart. Since those years in Kenya, our sons have grown, changed, and matured as well.

When I was a foreigner in Kenya, I longed for friends and connections with Africans. Our cultures were so extremely different. *What did we both enjoy?* I often wondered. Expensive gifts were not the answer. We would not always be there. How could I share God's love?

To those who seek, I believe God gives ways and ideas regarding how to connect. We are all unique. To each of us God gives ways to minister and to serve.

Plants and songs were connections for me. I have valued the beauty of plants everywhere I have lived. Extra baby plants were always coming up. Clippings were free, and they rooted easily. I dug, snipped, and carried plants with me when we visited friends. My African neighbors and friends were appreciative. I loved to see the bright splotches of color in their yards. Pineapple tops can grow with a bit of the fruit left on it. That was another gift they valued.

When I could not converse well in Luo, I pulled out my Luo songbook and sang with them in their language. The women taught me songs, and I hand-copied them in my tablet. They enjoyed hearing and learning songs in my language too.

Mark and I valued the traditional African songs. Right after Sunday School, we sang their songs by memory. When everyone went through the greeting line at church, they enthusiastically sang their African songs. Their songs are a beautiful part of their culture. It is a wonderful thing to love, notice, and appreciate the good.

To each of us God gives ways to minister and to serve.

༺∽༻

There is so much to glean in other cultures. We need the natives. We need their friendship and love. We learn from them.

In Kenya I was given the gift of friendship. With plants and with songs I shared care and beauty. The bird of paradise bloomed at just the right time, just when my sons would see it. I felt His love.

Wherever you go, leave beauty.

God, thank You so much for the beauties in Your wonderful creation, for the joy of music!

Read Luke 6:37-49

Mother's Reflections

Commit thy works unto the LORD, and thy thoughts shall be established. –Proverbs 16:3

Words from a new mom:

It's amazing, the picture I get of God's love. I love this baby because he is mine, not for anything he does [just as] God loves me. I don't have to do things just right for Him to love me and be pleased with me.

Getting my work done is starting to feel more manageable. But who knows, perhaps as soon as I say that, my day won't go so well. I was discouraged this morning. I told my husband I'm tired of racing around trying to get my work done. Even though my baby is better and getting over acid reflux, he isn't taking many long naps. When he's tired, he fights sleep so much that it takes forever to rock him to sleep. I enjoy my baby, but I also enjoy doing other things. Other things need to be done. People like to say to just enjoy your baby and spend time with him. What about eating? Can we wear dirty clothes? I go crazy if the house is messy.

> *"I need patience, prayers, and wisdom."*

This morning when talking to God, He reminded me that He gave me this baby. That is His perfect plan for my life. I want to learn in this stage and accept it even though there are hard aspects. I need patience, prayers, and wisdom.

On Friday, one of the single ladies stopped in with a gift for me and my new son. That meant something to me. I've tried to care about her.

Another mother I know had these words to say:

The children were all up before six this morning. I would so like some quiet moments before they're up each morning. I would have to get up at five. I have been praying that God would help all three of them sleep at the same time in the afternoon so I can read my Bible by myself. It is amazing how often they do sleep simultaneously now. It must be God answering because my best plans easily go awry. I have been encouraged.

Heart Search:

- Mother work is daily and demanding. Cry to God for His help and wisdom.
- View caring for family, teaching and encouraging children as a most important work for God.
- Am I willing to lay down my work and help others? Thinking of others brightens the day.
- I need to be a woman of the Word and of prayer.

Lord, help me take time to help others
and not just have a narrow view of only me.

Read 1 Timothy 5

A Living Sacrifice

Neither will I offer burnt offerings unto the LORD my God of that which doth cost me nothing. –2 Samuel 24:24

"My brother and his wife came home from Ghana at the end of March," a friend told me. "All of their six children were there to meet them at the airport along with five new grandchildren they had not yet seen. Another grandchild was born a few days after they returned."

Another friend confided, "I know about having new little grandsons when you are in a distant land. I cried when I heard that our son's first little child was born. I cried because I was happy. I cried because I wasn't there to see the new baby. I cried because I was sad I couldn't see my son as a father. God gives grace for those times. That little grandson is six now, and I enjoy him so much."

A relative said, "I remember how it felt for us—having the first three grandsons born in a two-month period before going to Belize. A grandchild was born the evening before we left early the next morning. I have to think of Luke 14:26: 'If any man come to me, and hate not his father, and mother, and wife, and children, and brethren, and sisters, yea, and his own life

Pray for missionaries as they give their lives as a living sacrifice. Pray for their children as they sacrifice at home.

also, he cannot be my disciple.' That verse helped us to gladly go for God's sake."

When Mark and I left for Africa, our first grandson was only three weeks old. It felt like we traveled a world away. God knows how many tears of loneliness I cried for our three oldest children, and the fact of missing out on our grandson's babyhood. That was part of our sacrifice for Jesus.

We think of sacrifices missionaries made out of love for Jesus. Do we consider that their married children at home are sacrificing as well? They cannot go to their parents' house for holidays. They miss the love and care of grandparents in the lives of their children. Phone calls could not easily be placed with the big time charges. They may be taking care of financial matters so parents can serve.

Pray for missionaries as they give their lives as a living sacrifice. Pray for their children as they sacrifice at home.

Jesus left the splendors of heaven because of love. What am I willing to do for Jesus?

Thank You, Jesus, for the gift and sacrifice of Your love.
I want to be willing to sacrifice for You.

Read Romans 12

Where I Am

My times are in thy hand: deliver me from the hand of mine enemies, and from them that persecute me. –Psalm 31:15

My daughters speak into my life and help me to think and process things in a good way. One day I said to them, "I feel like I am buried in Africa. I am so far away from family, old friends, and the familiar way of life back home in Ohio."

"Mom, I kept thinking about your comment of being buried in Africa. But mom, you aren't buried, you aren't dead. God sees you," my daughter encouraged. "I think being away from the rest of the family is what is the hardest for you. Or maybe in another sense, the Bible says we are buried with Him in baptism. I spend most of my hours on a windy ridge in the country with two small boys."

A young married lady shared at an Annual Ladies' Day. "It is hard to be at home with two little children," she commented. She encouraged the single ladies to appreciate their freedom.

My sister shared, "I am going through the 'Empty Nest Syndrome.' I am lonely, but that is where I am right now, and I must find contentment. It is so easy to look over at the greener grass on the other side of the fence. May we serve God joyfully right where we are!"

"May we serve God joyfully right where we are!"

We can sympathize with friends and show love and care. We

can encourage them to be thankful in present situations. While we were in Kenya, one of my friends reminded me to be grateful for the sons who were with us, rather than bemoaning the absence of grown children far away.

Ask God to help you enjoy your present stage of life. Don't allow life to pass you by with discontentment.

Isaiah 49:8-10 (NIV) is full of promises that comfort my heart. The Lord says:

- I will answer you.
- I will help you.
- I will keep you.
- I will guide you and have compassion.

God sees and understands each situation, even as He saw and cared about Hagar in her time of dire need.

Thank You, thank You for the wonderful promises in Your Word. Jesus, I want to love and trust You more.

Read Genesis 16

Warm and Welcoming

Finally, be ye all of one mind, having compassion one of another, love as brethren, be pitiful, be courteous.
–1 Peter 3:8

"There is no greater happiness for a man than approaching a door at the end of a day knowing someone on the other side of that door is waiting for the sound of his footsteps."[11] *–Ronald Reagan*

Andy and Nancy had a happy, satisfying marriage. He was glad when the workday was over and he could go home to a warm, welcoming woman.

Nancy shared, "When my husband Andy was diagnosed with cancer at age fifty-eight, I remember hoping the children would all be established and on their own before Andy's cancer took him. There were still three at home. We were not prepared for the news we got after a routine health screening. The doctor, after going over the results of the blood test, said it's either leukemia or multiple myeloma. We drove home in silence holding hands. This was a death to our dreams of growing old together, and possibly serving the Lord at Choice Books or Christian Light Education.

"God called us to share our faith at a cancer support group. God

---

[11] www.quotefancy.com

wanted us to be a witness at the cancer center and the few hospital stays.

"We shared, 'Andy will be a winner if he beats cancer or if he goes to be with Jesus.' Yet we would not have chosen this difficult ten-year journey of ill health.

"After Andy's death, a friend encouraged me to join a Grief Share Group. It was a huge help. The many emotions I was experiencing were normal and okay. I learned to cry out to God in my sorrow and loneliness. He heard me and held me up.

> *"I looked out the window and saw a beautiful rainbow. God was telling me, 'I am with you, and I will take care of you.'"*
>
> ∾

"One Saturday evening I was finishing in the kitchen. I had an intense longing for Andy to be here to sit with me and just to be together. An incredible lonely feeling flooded over me; my heart hurt. I was not sure how I could make it. I looked out the window and saw a beautiful rainbow. God was telling me, 'I am with you, and I will take care of you.' That was so precious and a great comfort. God's promises are true.

"There was a time I wished to die after Andy was gone. But when the hard grieving lessened, life had better days again. Now there are so many opportunities to serve others. I like to have quiet days at home too. God's grace is a wonderful thing, supplied when it is needed. God is with me. I am not alone."

God, help us love well and not take each other for granted.

Read Genesis 2:18-25

So Low

Judge not, and ye shall not be judged: condemn not, and ye shall not be condemned: forgive, and ye shall be forgiven.
–Luke 6:37

Luke 15 records the story of the prodigal son. This young man left home, spent his money on wild living, and then became destitute. He truly sunk to the lowest depths. He was desperately hungry, hungry enough to even consent to feed pigs. For a Jew, this was a great humiliation. To stoop even lower, so low as to eat the food the pigs touched, was to be degraded beyond belief. Moses's law clearly stated that pigs were unclean animals. They could not be eaten or used for sacrifices. They were not even to be touched.

The pig was a common sacrifice of pagan religions. God wanted Israel to be easily distinguished from heathen nations. A true Jew would not even stoop to touching a pig, lest he be defiled.

We were discussing this in family devotions. Micah said that even today pigs are disdained by Jews and Muslims. He read an account in *Sons of Hamas* where pigs were used on guard duty, instead of German Shepherd dogs, between two outer fences at a military base. The pigs were to serve as a psychological deterrent to any prospective terrorist who was a devout Muslim. Islam forbids contact with swine as vehemently as does Orthodox Judaism.

When a man, like the young prodigal, turns his back on God, things progressively get worse. One sin always leads to another, just as the prodigal broke many of God's commandments. He did not honor his parents and turned his back on God with the choices he made. When this young man came to his senses, repented, and returned home, his father lovingly welcomed him and forgave him all. The father forgave because he was filled with love. The eldest son was bitter and refused to forgive.

Each of us has a choice to either forgive those who wound and hurt us or to harbor bitterness and resentment.

Each of us has a choice to either forgive those who wound and hurt us or to harbor bitterness and resentment. Jesus enables us to forgive. He forgave the men who cruelly crucified Him. He forgives each one who comes to Him in true repentance.

Jesus forgives us no matter how low we have sunk. He forgives us when we have touched and fed filthy swine by committing horrible sins. His arms are ever ready to clean us up and lovingly welcome us home.

In the grace of forgiveness, imitate Jesus.

Forgiveness is possible with You, my Jesus.

Read Luke 15

Kenya Again

Serve the LORD with gladness: come before
his presence with singing. –Psalm 100:2

It was our last night at home before flying to Kenya to help at a youth Bible school. I was having such carnal thoughts. *God, you know I like my bed. It's so comfortable. I like my pillow too.* Another thought came to my head: "The Son of Man had no place to lay His head."

I like our shower. The head adjusts the water just right into a pleasant, warm, comfortable stream.

Remember: many in Kenya and other countries do not have running water.

I really do relish American foods. They are so handy, clean, and convenient. My freezer is full of fruits and vegetables and many kinds of meat. In Kenya, there are so many germs, even dung-smeared baskets containing food.

Be reminded: many are longing for more food.

Oh God, I give this long trip to you.

I am willing, Lord, to go to Kenya. I am willing. I will support Mark in ministries of music opportunities. I enjoy teaching young women and seeing many friends. It's been nearly a year since we left Kenya. I am privileged to travel there again. Many would love this opportunity. Going for three weeks is so much easier than three years, and it really does not seem so sacrificial.

We prayed for God to guide our steps and to make us a blessing. The trip was long and tiresome. The flights were exhausting. The first night we spent at a favorite guesthouse, "Amani" in Nairobi. God blessed us with sweet rest.

The days were packed full. From the Kisumu airport we drove with missionaries straight to Bible study and were greeted by many. The ladies told me I was fat. In Kenya, that is a compliment! We slept at the house in Ng'iya where we had lived. Solomon, the grounds man, was pleased to see us.

Singing the Swahili and Luo songs and connecting with many friends at the youth Bible school blessed our hearts. Dining with Freeman and Mary one evening at Top Cliff Restaurant, overlooking Lake Naivasha, was a meaningful time. I had the best paneer with rice. The chapatis were extra good. We enjoyed relating about life, missions, and families.

The first night we spent at a favorite guesthouse, "Amani" in Nairobi. God blessed us with sweet rest.

I thanked Jesus for this time in Kenya.

Thank you, Jesus, for the opportunity to serve.
Help us serve with gladness.

Read Matthew 24:32-51

He Weeps;
He Cares

*Thus saith the LORD, the God of David thy father, I have
heard thy prayer, I have seen thy tears.* –2 Kings 20:5

While at his funeral, an African lady was sharing a testimony about her deceased brother. She seemed to be on the verge of crying. The moderator noticed and remarked, "Christians don't need to cry."

Africans tend to be stoic; tears are squelched. But at their funerals, when shovels full of dirt rain on the coffin, the women will wail. A most mournful dirge goes on and on, sometimes until they fall over. Bystanders often have to keep them from falling into the grave.

If Christians should not cry, why did Jesus, when he was with Mary and Martha after Lazarus died, weep? Jesus saw Martha weeping. He heard their friends wailing. Jesus showed His care by weeping with them. The people standing nearby said, "See how much He loved him." We do not find Jesus reprimanding them for tears or for wailing.

In the days when Jesus walked on earth, there was a popular Greek concept of God. In this Greek view, God was portrayed as unemotional and detached from any messy involvement with humans.

God is personal and caring. He cares so much that He is touched and weeps in our sorrows. In the story of Lazarus, we see Jesus expressing emotions of compassion, indignation, and sorrow. He often expressed deep emotions.

God wants us, His children, to reveal our true feelings to Him. He understands. Jesus was God on earth and experienced what we do, all without sinning. God knows and His heart is full of compassion, love, and care.

We were made to share. We were not made to keep our hurts all bottled up alone in our hearts. If I

God wants us, His children, to reveal our true feelings to Him.

am not willing to share struggles with friends, how can they weep with me? When my brother, who was mentally ill, passed away, it was healing for me to share the news with close friends in church. I needed their prayers, comfort,

and love. My sharing opened the door for some of them to talk about painful situations in their own families. Each one of us has wounds and difficult situations. Sharing aids in healing.

We need tears. We need each other. Tears are the words the heart cannot express.

Thank You, God, that You are a God of comfort.
I run to You for shelter.

Read John 11:17-44

Too Comfortable

*For God so loved the world, that he gave his only begotten
Son, that whosoever believeth in him should not perish,
but have everlasting life.* –John 3:16

"I called Mirna, my dear friend in El Salvador," Margretta
shared. "I have thirty free minutes every month to make an
international call. I hadn't called her in a long time as my
phone plan just started offering that recently."

Abel and Mirna's family is living in Las Delicias. They do not
plan to work at the school for deaf children in another area, like we
had heard. They were asked to go
there, and Mirna said she would
have liked to for one year, but they
wanted a three-year commitment.
Abel was really into it, but Mirna's heart was in their home village, Las Delicias. They took into
consideration that all their needs
would be supplied. Financially, it
would be a life of ease, with plenty
of good food and money at the deaf school. They were afraid they
would get too comfortable and not want to leave that place.

*God reached out to the
darkness of this world
by sending the Light,
His Son Jesus.*

"I felt that was definitely very noble," Margretta said. "Our flesh
longs for a life of comfort."

Mirna talked of a neighbor lady whom she recently showed the
way to the Lord before she died. She spoke of another lady she was
visiting every day.

Though the large village where they live seems like a stronghold of Catholicism, they are being faithful and encouraged in the work. Abel, Mirna, and their family are a witness for Jesus in their homeland of El Salvador.

God reached out to the darkness of this world by sending the Light, His Son Jesus.

- The apostle Paul invested his life and energy to bring people to Jesus.
- To whom do I reach out?
- Do I care about anyone?
- There are lonely people in our churches.
- We all have neighbors.
- What am I willing to sacrifice to share the love of Jesus?

May sharing Jesus, not comfort, be your goal. Listen to His voice and promptings.

Jesus, show me how to share your love and care.

Read John 10:22-42

Never Alone

I am not alone, because the Father is with me. –John 16:32

"How would it be to live alone? How difficult it would be to be a widow," worried Clara. The thought of living alone was her worst fear.

Saturday morning was Atlee and Clara's thirty-third anniversary. He wished her a happy anniversary. Their marriage was solid, founded on the Rock of Jesus; it was satisfying and good. Did he appreciate his wife more than many men do? He had been a widower for twenty years before he met and married Clara. His first wife had passed away from acute leukemia, and he had been left with five young children.

But this thirty-third anniversary day was difficult. Atlee had a massive stroke that very day and was rushed by the squad to the hospital. He was there for seven days. Clara was at his side most of the time. The doctor finally told the family a feeding tube could be put in to prolong life, or they could take him home and make him comfortable. His family knew their husband and dad was ready to go home to Jesus. They had often heard him say to not prolong life if health failed. His speech was affected, but he had whispered to Clara, "I love you," and he had clearly told her, "I heard angels sing." Those words brought joy and gladness to her heart.

Hospice had everything ready when they brought him home. Atlee relaxed and slept. On Saturday evening, he held Clara's hand tightly as she stood by his bedside. Gradually, his hold relaxed. He could not speak while his wife and family watched over him. His breathing became more shallow; a few times he smiled. At twenty past ten, he passed away with a smile on his face. Clara knew without a doubt that her Atlee was home with Jesus.

Their family room was a special spot where they had read the Word and prayed each morning. Their custom was to read the Word again in the evening. He always thanked the Lord that they had another day together when they prayed at bedtime. In that room he drew his last breath.

Yet even through her tears, she felt a sweet presence come over her.

∽

Wednesday was the funeral. The day was difficult, but Clara felt God's love and care through the support of family and many friends. By Thursday evening the family had all gone home. "Though alone, I had to go in the family room," Clara shared. She went in and sat down. Then tears flooded her eyes, and she sobbed brokenly. Yet even through her tears, she felt a sweet presence come over her. It was Jesus. She knew it was! The fear all drained out of her, tears ceased, and a calmness filled her heart. She glanced at the clock. It was fifteen past nine. She prayed, and all fear was gone. God gave her sweet rest that night. The next evening, she went in the family room. Again, she felt the same presence of God at fifteen minutes past nine.

"God has given me grace right when I needed it. I have felt His presence often through the years since Atlee's death," she shared. "God is with me, though living alone, I am not alone, and I am not afraid. Isaiah 49:16 is a comfort to me: 'Behold, I have graven thee upon the palms of my hands; thy walls are continually before me.'"

I appreciate my husband, God Almighty;
help me to never take him for granted.

Read Psalm 23

Africa and America

Africa is Africa;
America is America.
In between is ten thousand miles.
Africa seems to be a different planet.

New people in missions
 have fresh ideas and inspirations.
Those that have been there for years
 have practical experience.

New people trust and love everyone.
Seasoned missionaries are tempted
 to become cynical and hardened,
 with trials of deceptions.

Can the fresh new people
 and the experienced missionaries,
Graciously accept each other
and live and work in peace?

Can we love each other
 as children of the same Father?

Will we learn with humility?
Affirm and encourage each other?

Or will we be threatened
 over new gifts and talents?
Will jealousy close our eyes
 to working together well for Jesus?

Africa is Africa;
America is America.
In between is ten thousand miles
 and vast cultural differences.
Lord, help us to love and learn.

EPILOGUE

Rest in Life's Seasons

This article first appeared in *Daughters of Promise* magazine, Issue 28, 2019.

I n my heart is (and has been) a deep longing to enjoy each season of life, to be faithful and useful for Jesus. I don't want to live for tomorrow, but to embrace today, with my face toward the Son. I have faced difficult things and still do. I know God is good to me. He is with me.

In the House of a Husband

One summer evening thirty-four years ago, Mark and I were on our front porch poring over the Sunday School lesson. I loved our life of togetherness with God and each other. That day, the verse in Ruth 1:9 intrigued me: "The LORD grant you that ye may find rest [security, permanent home], each of you in the house of her husband." I found rest when newly married, for I need continued rest with Jesus and with my husband. A friend encouraged me when I was a young woman to pray daily for my husband for wisdom to lead our home. Praying that prayer has been a reminder to trust and rest.

Season at Home

I gazed at our tiny newborn daughter. What a precious gift. After nearly three years of marriage and a miscarriage, I was thrilled to have this baby. I felt ready and happy to be at home.

I could not know that when this little miss turned five, we would have our fourth child. The year we had four preschoolers was one of the most busy and demanding years of my life. I coped better by being at home a lot, especially during afternoons when our little ones needed their naps.

Reading, writing, and resting when the house was quiet refreshed my mind. There were days, though, when the two who were fifteen months apart did not nap at the same time. There were nights when sleep was interrupted. The care of small ones was a daily constant.

I did not always cope well with unexpected pregnancies and wondered how I would survive. Even that struggle put me on a senseless guilt trip. Prayer, surrender to God's will, and candidly sharing as a couple and with other women was helpful. Each baby needs and deserves to be wanted and loved. God always eventually brought me to that place of acceptance and rest.

The words of Mary ministered to my soul: "I am the Lord's servant and will do what He desires" (Luke 1:38 paraphrase).

It was easy to wonder, in the midst of crying babies, dirty diapers, and dishes, if anything I am doing really matters! It is easy to get bogged down in the mundaneness of ordinary work.

One day when I was preparing for guests, my small daughter sweetly said, "Mama, you need to ask Jesus to help you." Ah, children keep us humbled—so aware of how much we need God.

Mothering is a big work for God. Don't buy into the lie that you are not doing much for Him while spending years at home with little ones. Your life will affect your children for eternity. In this season at home, there is rest by accepting the work and duties of raising children for Jesus. I looked for the sunshine in each season, appreciated my faithful husband's love, and the affections and delights of my children.

I packed lunches and was a teacher's wife for years. There is much value in embracing my husband's calling. The years of everyone at home, family trips, and young adults in the house were a special time in life that has flown by on the wings of time. They seem now like a streak in time, a blur in my mind. I am grateful for all the times we worked, played, traveled, sang, and prayed with our children. No parent regrets time spent with one's children.

Weddings and Grandchildren

Two beautiful daughters leave us. Two weddings nine months apart. They moved far away to start their own homes. We had worked side-by-side for years. Though I knew it was all in God's plan, the adjustment was not easy. Three months after the second wedding, we uprooted and left for Kenya.

Half of us there, daughters in America, a son in El Salvador. A three-week-old first grandson. The transition was difficult. A scattered family is a sacrifice. The will of God is often not an easy breeze. There was much to do and many unending needs in Africa. Some days I just needed to stay at home. Quietness and rest before God was so vital.

We worked, we learned, and we made many friends in Kenya. Now, for the past three years, America has been home again.

Winds of Change

Is my rest in God secure? With the winds of change ever blowing, blowing, will I revel in my love for Jesus? As my children no longer need me so much, will I be a blessed sweet influence for Jesus? It is easy to have my heart so entwined with my children, my sense of worth too bound up in them. With adult children in the house, I need to continually let go, let go, let go as they come and go. When my children were small, I could fix many things. With adult children, it is not simple. I cannot fix their issues. They may not even care for my advice.

When I ask a child a question that shows concern, what will I do when I receive a snide remark in return? Sometimes I just want to fall over and wail, "God, I don't know how to mother well in this stage." Hours later, my wounded heart praises God that my child's heart is soft enough to offer an apology.

I plead for wisdom. I am determined to learn, not to despair when the way is difficult.

In times of turmoil, I find rest in the words of Jesus. Chapter after chapter. In the dark, in the light, until my heart is rested. When my mind is troubled, pouring out my prayers on paper rests my mind.

If my expectations are for a trouble-free life, I will fall into despair. Recently, singing "Somewhere in the Skies" ministered to my soul. Our eternal home will be the perfect place where nothing goes wrong; it will be paradise forever. I always like something to look forward to. As the years go by, I have an anticipation for home. I am also grateful my Savior is here to help me today.

There is joy and rest in God through every season.

Right now, a small lad with the darkest, brightest eyes quietly sits on my lap. We are watching for birds at the feeder.

"Come, eat," the little boy calls. I am singing songs about birds. We read stories. I enjoy this grandmothering ritual.

The enemy whispers blackly in my ear, "You were not a good parent like this."

"In Jesus's name, go away thou destroyer of rest and peace, thou father of lies," I pray.

I was not a perfect mother, but I dearly loved my children. I remember our house filled with songs. We cuddled and read on many days. My goal was daily Bible stories; countless other books were devoured.

My daughter and her family came to visit in the summertime. It's a comfort to have her here, especially since my house is ever full of men.

I felt discouraged when she left. I needed to get out of the house. Walking and praying fight the blues. I do want to be content in this season of so many changes.

On days when my mind wants to run on negative tracks, will I fill the house with music, open my mouth and sing, even when I do not feel like singing? Listening to inspirational podcasts helps me focus on truth. Taking time to connect with other women is vital. These things help me enjoy and rest today.

I love quiet mornings. God has given me the strong desire for aloneness with Him for so many years. My heart is grateful. Precious mornings with Jesus are a vital part of rest, and I am strengthened when the first thing I reach for in the morning is the life-giving words of Jesus. I am determined to give Jesus, not technology, not my phone, priority in the morning.

I was singing with a large group, directed by my husband. The words of the song "Somewhere in the Skies" washed over my being. Nothing goes wrong there, and we will feel so glad and free when in paradise forever.

Oh Jesus, life is ever full of changes and difficult things. This world we live in is so fallen. Thank You that through it all, You whisper sweet peace and rest.

It's a cool morning. A man and his wife, their hair streaked with gray, sit side by side, reading the precious Word. We read and sang with our children for many years. Now it is often the two of us. There is joy and rest in God through every season.

IF YOU'RE A FAN OF THIS BOOK, WILL YOU HELP ME SPREAD THE WORD?

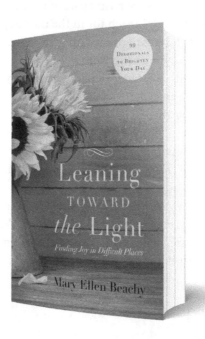

There are several ways you can help me get the word out about the message of this book…

- Post a 5-Star review on Amazon.
- Recommend the book to friends – word-of-mouth is still the most effective form of advertising.
- Purchase additional copies to give away as gifts.

The best way to connect with me is by email:
maryellenbeachy@icloud.com

ENJOY THESE OTHER BOOKS
BY MARY ELLEN BEACHY

Children Around the World
Thirty-eight character-building stories from around the world

In *Children Around the World*, learn from stories from numerous countries and Kenya. And above all, God's strength and miracles in the midst of very difficult times.

Illustrated. Paperback. 180 pg. $9.99 + shipping

Title: Hearing God in Ordinary Days
Author: Mary Ellen Beachy

In *Hearing God in Ordinary Days*, Mary Ellen Beachy encourages daily seeking God in solitude. She gives practical advice about finding joy in the ordinary.

240 pages. 5 1/2"x 8 1/2". Softcover. $10.99 + shipping

Title: Women At the Cross
Subtitle: Discovering the
Work of the Cross in the Lives of 12 Women of the Bible - for Today's Woman
Author: Mary Ellen Beachy

What I learned from 12 women of the Bible, and 12 contemporary women.

193 pages. 5 1/2"x 8 1/2". Softcover. $10.99 + shipping.

You can order these books from:
Mary Ellen Beachy
maryellenbeachy@icloud.com

CPSIA information can be obtained
at www.ICGtesting.com
Printed in the USA
LVHW021748041021
699499LV00008B/390

9 781954 533134